YOUR DREAMS AND YOU

IVANIA ALVARADO

Your Dreams and You
First English edition
© 2021 by Ivania Alvarado

ISBN-13: 978-1-7375602-4-1

Original Spanish Version: *Los Sueños y Usted*
First Edition: Biblioteca Jurídica Diké 29/02/2004
Translated by Joseph Montes
Barcelona, Spain

All rights reserved. No part of this book may be used or reproduced by any means, graphic, electronic, or mechanical, stored in a database including photocopying, recording, taping or by any information storage retrieval system without the written permission of the publisher except in the case of brief quotations embodied in critical articles and reviews.

Contents

Acknowledgments ... 9
Introduction ... 10
CHAPTER I: Dreams ... 13
    Meanings and the unknown ... 13
    What are they for and why do we dream? ... 14
    Recurring Dreams ... 15
    Dreams lacking importance ... 15
    Steps to follow for improving our way
        of interpreting dreams ... 16
    What are the best dreams? ... 18
    Biblical Dreams ... 21
    Joseph's dreams ... 22
    One dream, different meanings ... 25
CHAPTER II: Optimism in dreams ... 27
    How to achieve a change in position
        with the help of our dreams ... 28
    How dreams can benefit your daily life. ... 29
    Negative dream turned into positive ... 30

Changing the direction of the dream
    so it doesn't happen to you ... 31
How we can explain it to them ... 33
Dreams that warn of coming conflicts,
    problems or gossip ... 35
Warning dreams ... 36
Who is sending us these warning
    messages and why? ... 38
"Messages", path that reaches the end,
    you have to turn back or stay there ... 39
Encouraging dreams and messages ... 40
When that person consulted with me,
    I said to them ... 41

CHAPTER III: Darkness and Nightmares ... 43
    Dreams that on occasion mean death ... 46
    Dream of the death of someone
        but it means something else ... 48

CHAPTER IV: Experiences and wishes ... 51
    Dreams in the past, present and future ... 52
    Dream that reflects financial improvement ... 54
    Dreams with money ... 57

CHAPTER V: Fantasies, sex, romance,
    kisses in dreams ... 59
    Dream about an artist ... 61
    Infidelity in dreams ... 62
    Seeing your rival ... 63

Dictionary of dreams and their lucky number ... 65
    Letter A ... 66
    Letter B ... 74
    Letter C ... 82
    Letter D ... 91
    Letter E ... 96
    Letter F ... 100
    Letter G ... 109
    Letter H ... 114
    Letter I ... 119
    Letter J ... 122

Letter K	125
Letter L	128
Letter M	133
Letter N	138
Letter O	142
Letter P	146
Letter Q	151
Letter R	152
Letter S	157
Letter T	167
Letter U	173
Letter V	175
Letter W	177
Letter X	183
Letter Y	185
Letter Z	187
The Author	189
Dreams diary and its use	193

Acknowledgments

God, Who has given me the opportunity to express what I have inside.

My parents, José and Mariah, who taught me love and unconditional kindness.

My children, Sophia, Stephanie, and Alexander, who are my inspiration every day.

My siblings, Raquel and Armando. Their unconditional support showed me the path of truth.

A special mention to those who have collaborated and trusted me for the interpretation of their dreams.

Introduction

Dreams and their interpretation have been a topic that has puzzled and interested humanity for thousands of years, before Christ to the present.

Regardless of religion, culture or nationality, as humans we want to know why we dream and if our dreams are useful. Whether old or young, we all dream.

For centuries, many people have considered their dreams to be revelations that are no more than a manifestation of a secret and hidden truth.

Who is sending us these messages? Why? Is it our subconscious? Our hidden wishes? Or perhaps it's intelligence from beyond?

I wrote this book to help you interpret your own dreams. I hope you share your experiences with friends, family, or your partner, but especially with your children. This could be an excellent way to have something in common with your kids and find out if they are having any problems, whether someone is bothering them in school, or if they are having a drug problem. All of these issues are reflected in nightmares.

I'd also like to change the negative way you might interpret some dreams, especially if you say:

> This is a bad, ugly dream.
> I didn't like it so I'm not going to interpret it.

To a certain degree, you're right, because what you wish for in life generally comes true. At the same time, if you have a more open mind, you can interpret that dream, even if it made you lose sleep or it shocked you so much you don't want to remember it. If you can confront it, it will help you differentiate between what's real and what isn't.

The majority of dreams we don't like are "warning dreams." Because of this, you *must* interpret them to get to the message. In this book, I mention certain warning dreams the dreamer may not like, and I will share one of my "warning dreams" I had when I was 9 that repeated until I was 19.

In my recurring dream, I saw my father dying. Because I want to get everything positive from what God gives me that I can, I wanted to understand the importance of this recurring dream.

This dream helped me understand that I, as the eldest daughter, had to learn from life to prepare for what was coming. The dream was my key to resolving that problem. In the end, my father didn't die, but there was a complete 180 degree change in my family's life.

After interpreting a dream you don't like, you take the positive, throw away the negative, and only recollect in your mind what you have to do so it won't come true.

These types of dreams are not only warnings but obtained experiences without having lived them in real life. At the same time, they are like a vaccine for what's coming, so the experience can be gentler or pass more smoothly.

We can manage and control our dreams to make them more positive, in our favor. We can use them to change the path of things, by turning an ugly or bad dream into something positive.

In this book, for some of the dreams, I will analyze them from a completely personal viewpoint.

Lastly, we must take advantage of our own dreams. There have been many writers, inventors, businesspeople, and others who have made money from dreams.

The psychologist Carl Jung said when we have dreams that are never erased from our minds, they are "Great Dreams," when we learn to appreciate their meaning. They're the "most precious jewels in the mine of our soul."

CHAPTER I
Dreams

Meanings and the Unknown

What are they for and why do we dream?

All human beings dream, just like animals. The difference between how animals and humans dream is that we spend most of the time in the Rapid Eye Movement phase.

Most of our dreams, especially those we remember, the ones that are most transcendental happen in the REM phase. We all need to enter this phase and dream to help the development and function of our brain.

When we sleep at night, we generally enter this phase two to three times. In REM, the heart and circulatory system accelerate. The nervous system produces intense discharges of energy that accelerates the circulatory rhythm.

According to scientists, all humans need to enter the REM phase. This is the time our body repairs itself and processes the day's ideas and memories.

Why do we dream and what are they for? This is the question we ask ourselves when we wake up and remember a dream. Scientists haven't been able to answer this question completely. The truth is that dreams are like puzzles. We have to study them and put them together piece by piece to get to the result or answer.

We have to interpret them, because if we dream it can't be for nothing. There must be a reason and the reason is important to our progress and development. We need it for growth and daily enrichment, to understand part of life in our world when we're awake.

Recurring Dreams

We have to pay more attention to recurring dreams, for they could be signaling important things to us, perhaps to help us in our transcendence and to tell us something that can benefit us. They're sending us a message. Because we aren't paying attention, it's repeated several times until the opportunity or danger passes or we pay attention.

Dreams lacking importance

1. Dreams with people, things, or events we heard of or experienced recently.

2. Dreams that happen in the first hours we fall asleep, as the brain is still busy with digestion.

3. Nightmares because of something we've seen, read in a book, pain, or a matter that worries us.

4. Dreams that result from a bad sleeping posture; we are pressuring an organ.

5. Dreams provoked by an illness that we have or is coming.

6. Dreams caused by the external environment such as noise, cold, etc.

7. Dreams that are caused by medication, drugs, too much food, too little or bad digestion.

*Steps to follow for improving
our way of interpreting dreams.*

There are many ways to interpret dreams, but one way is to divide your dreams into different parts and elements. Then you can go back and identify your desire and what you want to do.

To begin with, you will need a notebook or diary on your nightstand, this book, a pencil, a lamp, and a glass of water. Water is one of the richest minerals that exists, and it helps us cleanse our own energy.

Second, you must try not to open your eyes when you wake up. Instead, think about what you dreamed and gather what you saw in the dream from beginning to end and what you felt. Then open your eyes slowly and write down what you dreamed.

It's very important to identify what you feel when you wake up, whether you had a nice dream, or a dream you didn't like at all. You may have had a dream with no meaning at all, for example: If you wake up happy, sad, or frustrated but have no context for the emotion.

What you feel in the dream is one of the main parts, because it will help you interpret for what you feel is your sixth sense, your third eye that saw and felt what you didn't see or remember.

When you dream and wake up, you will never remember 100% of the dream. There are people who dream of death and don't necessarily feel bad when they wake up.

Some dreams are the opposite of what they seem. If you dream of death, it means life, and points to drastic changes in your life. Because of this, it's very important to highlight what you feel, the colors you see, and the objects in your dream. As you write, identify the subject of the dream, the main part of the dream, and the message.

What does an object mean? Whether it's a tree, a stranger, a person you know, dead or alive, identify the object, because interpreting the dream requires all of its parts.

Start by identifying the main theme of the dream. Record what impressed you, what you liked, and what you didn't like about the dream, how you woke up, and what feeling you woke up with.

After that, divide the dreams in colors and the objects you're seeing. Then you can analyze them. It's very important to identify a dream and analyze it the same day. If it isn't useful the same day, it doesn't matter. The important thing is to write them down, because if you don't, you might forget.

Your memory will try to put your dreams together with other dreams, and you won't be able to tell them apart. Here's an example: in the early morning, a dream makes you wake up. It's important to write it down, but not interpret it right then, because it can make you lose sleep. Write it down or record it, if you have a recorder, and interpret it the next day after you wake up.

The sooner you interpret it, the better. As you interpret more and more dreams, you will get better at it, because you'll go straight to the objective. You will know what you feel, what the subject is, what the primordial side is, when you begin to interpret your dreams.

Remember: not all dreams are real. As you interpret them, you'll learn more about the topic.

What are the best dreams?

Some of the exercises I recommend are more advanced. In later chapters, I'll share other works as a reference.

To have more enjoyable dreams, it's important to have a calm mind, forgiving your enemies, wishing the best to every possible human being, and no harm to anyone. If you do that, you will always have beautiful dreams. Go to sleep with a tranquil mind so the vibrations of the cosmos can enter your room and the light of the universe illuminates you.

If you read at night, you might later dream about what you read. It can influence your sleep. It depends on what you are reading.

If you're going to read something and don't want to have bad dreams, logically you shouldn't read horror novels or watch similar films. Instead, choose a neutral book that doesn't alter your nervous system. That's why it's good to take into account the dreams that happen in the early morning. Your brain will be more relaxed, and interpretation of the dream will be improved.

There is a preferred way to interpret and remember your dreams and there is also a best time to do so.

Between one and two in the morning and six or seven, is when the brain, the mind, the body, and the soul connect more to your spiritual side. The body is more rested and can assimilate the energies better and have more productive dreams. For example:

Dreams at the beginning of the night can be lazy dreams that have no meaning at all. The brain is still occupied with other matters that are necessary for the functioning of the nervous system.

Dreams in which we drink something with alcohol, drugs, or medications, we eat too much, are ill, some kind of decomposition of the body due to temperature, whether it's a slight illness, a dream related to something we talked about with someone, or went to sleep thinking about something.

When you dream of something related to what you were thinking, it will be reflected in your dream.

If you're going through something big in your life and are thinking about that, what you heard, what you said, dreamed, did, and why you did it, don't take those types of dreams too seriously.

Other types of people are more advanced in directing their dreams. They can go to sleep and say they want to dream about something or someone who is in their past or present.

You can develop this. Dream and think of what you want or must do. You can program yourself and order your subconscious when you go to sleep and say your prayers.

First think about what you want to program and what the message is you wish to send. Be clear on what you want to ask.

It can be a goal or a desired achievement. Ask your subconscious to dream what you want to dream and that way obtain the desired answer, connecting yourself through telepathy with reference to one person in particular.

You'll be able to know what they want, if they wish to harm you or are thinking about you; if you are in love with someone and want to know how they feel, you can connect through telepathy with them.

This exercise has very good results: If you are in your bed completely relaxed and the person you wish to send a message telepathically to is sleeping at that moment, make a mental effort to focus and visualize towards them, transmitting the energy you wish to send. You can know what that other person is dreaming or thinking.

Some people dream about their childhood home, when they were children in their home country, or the fond memories of their past they don't want to forget. Dreams like this help repair past emotions.

In this part of the exercise, the individual needs to return to their childhood or the start of the situation that caused the trauma or pain and repair what was left inconclusive.

It is important to go back in your mind and be able to realize what you missed and what you need to help yourself.

Biblical Dreams

We've been talking about dreams. What are they? Are they premonitions, visions, revelations... The truth is that even in the Bible dreams are mentioned.

Dreams are recorded in the Old and New Testaments. Here are some of the most notable biblical dreams:

God appears to Jacob in Bet-el (Genesis 28:12-16). The vision Jacob had was about the stairway to heaven: "I have here a ladder, that was supported on the ground, the other end touched Heaven; and I have here the angels of God that went up and down the ladder, who said: I'm Jehovah, the God of Abraham, your father and God of Isaac: the Earth in which he is resting, I will give it to you and your descendants. Your offspring will be like dust on the ground, and you will reach the West, East, South and North; all families are Earth will be blessed in you and in your seed. I am with you, and it will save you wherever you go, and I will bring you again to this Earth; because I won't leave you until I do what I've told you. And Jacob woke up from his dream and said: 'Clearly, Jehovah is here, and I did not know.'"

Joseph's dreams

"Joseph is sold by his brothers" (Genesis 37:3-11). Israel was the father who loved Joseph the most, for he was his youngest son, whom he had at an old age. Joseph's older brothers were jealous because he was the favorite. His father even made a tunic in various colors especially for Joseph. His brothers didn't like that. Joseph was a 17-year-old who shepherded sheep and had the ability to receive revelations from God through his dreams and interpretations. He had two dreams before his brothers first tried to kill him and then, because they weren't brave enough to go through with it, they sold him to the Israelis that took him to Egypt as a slave.

This is Joseph's dream: "I dreamed we were tying bunches in the middle of the field and that my bunch would stand up straight and that yours would come around and would be inclined to mine."

His brothers responded, "Will you reign over us?" And they loathed him more because of his dreams.

He had another dream and he told his brothers and then his father, "I have here the sun and the moon and eleven stars that inclined towards me."

The father replied, "What kind of dream is this? Do you think I, your mother, and your brothers will bow down to you?"

Then his brothers sold him. Potiphar, a captain of the Pharaoh's guard, bought him.

Joseph interprets two dreams (Genesis 40:8-22). Joseph, now in prison, knows the boss of the Pharaoh's cupbearers and the chief of bakers. He interpreted their dreams:

They said to him, "We've had a dream who no one can interpret."

Joseph said, "Aren't they God's interpretations? Tell me now."

The head of cupbearers said: "I dreamed I saw a vine in front of me. In the vine there were three branches, and its grapes were becoming ripe. The Pharaoh's cup was in my hand and I would take the grapes and squeeze them in the cup, and I would then give the Pharaoh the cup."

Joseph said, "The three branches are three days. In three days, the Pharaoh will lift your head and substitute you, and you will give him the cup as you did before as a simple cupbearer. Remember me when you have this chance, and I beg you that you have mercy with me and mention me to the Pharaoh and take me out of this house."

The chief of bakers said to Joseph, "I also dreamed that I saw three baskets over my head. In the highest basket, there were all kinds of pastries for the Pharaoh. The birds would eat them off the baskets on my head."

Joseph replied, "The three baskets are three days. In three days, the Pharaoh will take your head off your shoulders, will hang it, and the birds will eat off the flesh."

Joseph interpreted the Pharaoh's dream (Genesis 41:15-28). The Pharaoh said to Joseph, "In my dream it seemed as if I was at the shore of the river; the river would lift seven cows of beautiful appearance, that prance around the field, and seven other cows would go up after them, but these were thin and of horrible appearance. I've never seen such ugly cows in the land of Egypt. The ugly thin cows would eat the first fat cows, but you wouldn't know because the appearance of the cows stayed the same. I woke up. The next day I had another dream. Seven spikes were growing on a cane, other seven smaller and ugly spikes were growing after them and the small ones would devour the big beautiful ones."

Joseph responded, "The dream of the Pharaoh is one: God has shown the Pharaoh what he's going to do. The seven beautiful cows are seven years, and the spikes are too. The seven thin cows and small spikes mean seven years of hunger."

Just like the interpretations of biblical dreams, some dreams are more than just a simple dream.

There are many other examples of biblical dreams, like the one about Joseph dreaming of the birth of Jesus Christ (Matthew 1:18-21; 2:12-14. 19-21, 27:17-20). In many other dreams, Jehovah appeared to Moses and the prophets. The wife of Pilate had revelatory dreams and would beg her husband to save Christ and many others. These are not only biblical but historical occurrences.

Are these dreams prophetic? Use your intuition and ask your inner self. You'll have the answer.

One dream, different meanings

When I say the same dream can have different meanings, it's because one dream doesn't mean the same thing for everyone. Simply put, a dream can mean something different for someone else. You'll have to ask yourself, if you are going through a problem at the moment, if your dream applies to your current situation. If you're a professional, usually your dreams reflect on your work or business. If you're a housewife, it will reflect on your family. If you're a young person, it reflects school or anxiety you might have. If you dream about yourself taking an exam at school, or if you dream about your anxieties, you might be going through an issue. You must analyze the problem and figure out how to resolve it.

CHAPTER II

Optimism in dreams

How to achieve a change in position with the help of our dreams

When we talk about dreams, I like to include something positive. For instance, you can say, "I'm going to change my life, improve it, and do things better. I'm going to make my dreams come true."

Many people mistakenly think that being successful means having money; however, I believe being successful means achieving our dreams, when we can say, "I achieved what I wanted. I achieved what I was dreaming." In this book of dreams, I will include a bit of positivity, because I don't want it to be just a dictionary of dreams and how to interpret them, but also how to make your dreams positive.

Dreams don't remain only scenes, memories, or interpretations. The dreams you like can be made your reality, like the dream when you saw an artist and said you wanted to be an artist. You can do it. Why would you think otherwise? If you want to be a great model, why not? You must believe you can be a great author. You can be successful in business. After all, why couldn't you have your own business?

To improve your life and change the way you dream you will need to wash your brain. If you want to be successful in life, change on the inside and believe you are capable of doing anything you put your mind to do. I included this short exercise for you to do every night before going to bed:

Write your goals on a piece of paper (be sure to include both long-term and short-term goals). Make sure they're realistic and possible, and record what you have to do to achieve them.

1. Read them aloud every night when you pray or meditate before you go to sleep.

2. Tell yourself you'll have more positive dreams, especially dreams that can help you in your day-to-day life.

3. Analyze every dream you have. Determine what you didn't like, then change it to something positive. For instance, if someone is following you in your dreams, ask them questions like: Why are you following me? What message do you have for me? If you do this exercise every day, you will start to believe you are capable of achieving anything you set our mind to. You won't be afraid to tell your dreams to others, because you'll be sure you can achieve them. The most important thing is to believe it first yourself. With this you will have achieved the first 80%. You will only need the last 20%, which is to take action. Repeat this activity every night and take advantage of every dream you have.

How dreams can benefit your daily life.

Dreams enrich your life. You don't have to go through certain experiences if you've already lived them in a dream. If you had a dream you didn't enjoy, it's fine. Learn something positive from that dream so it doesn't happen again. Many people are afraid to decipher dreams they don't like because they fear the dreams will come true, but that's not the way it happens. If you have a dream you don't like, it doesn't mean it's going to happen. You can decide the dream doesn't belong to you, that it's not going to happen to you or your family, or anyone on the planet.

Dreams can help you meditate on your life and put your ideas in order. Maybe you did something or said something that offended someone. You may not have realized it, but if you have a dream as that person, you'll realize you've made a mistake. Dreams also enrich your ideas if you are a writer. If you're an entrepreneur, they will reveal ways to improve your business.

Negative dreams turned into positive ones

As you interpret your dreams, take the positive part of the dreams that will benefit you, those dreams that may work for your good. But beware! Not all dreams you don't like are useless, for everything in life has two sides to it: a negative and a positive. Which side are you on?

Every dream has two sides, and you should only interpret the positive side. Even negative dreams can help you change your mentality, how you can improve based on your dreams, and how to use those energies to get out the most positive in you.

Dreams related to accidents are sometimes warnings. They ask you to pay more attention to what you're doing. You have to change how you do things or how you see them. The same dream won't mean the same for everyone; you'll need to use your sixth sense to interpret it. If the dream was about an accident, you will have different ways of interpreting it. If you are going through problems, these problems can be reflected in the accident. If you don't have any issues, the dream can be seen positively, and you can take consider things you may have missed because you are distracted. Realize your deam may be a tool to prevent something from happening again, to make you more prepared the next time. Don't think negatively, but be prepared for anything. For instance, in the United States we are a very prepared country. We don't have to go to war to be prepared with an army.

Simply put, you need to be prepared, just in case something happens. Accidents can also be a reference point if you have recently seen one. This is your subconscious trying to speak to you.

*Changing the direction of the dream
so it doesn't happen to you*

One time I had a dream that woke me up in shock: I was in my car with my sister, her children, and my children. What happened? We fell off a bridge. We were driving to Miami Beach, and we fell from the bridge. We were about to crash into some boats; it happened so suddenly, and I immediately thought: "If I had something to break the glass, this would not be happening." Logically, in the dream it was going to happen, but at that moment I was thinking, "If this car sinks in such deep water, how can we get out alive?" That worried me.

If I weren't a positive person, I would have thought, "This is a bad dream and I don't want it to happen to me. I won't allow it in my mind and I will eliminate it." To the contrary, I took that dream and used it positively.

I told my family, "You know we live in Florida. We are surrounded by water, canals, lakes, and the ocean. We all need to have something in our cars to break the glass if we were to be trapped underwater. We hear on the news about how people fall into water with their cars. Some drown and some survive, but what happens if we don't have the tools to be able to save ourselves or our children?" In the dream, this was presented as a sign of need, not only of my own but of everyone. From this dream, I took on maximum positivity and patented that invention.

Children dream too. How can we help them when they have nightmares and teach them about the importance of sharing dreams?

When we are children, according to scientists, we spend most of our sleep time dreaming. As we grow, the number of dreams we remember starts to diminish. When we are older, we usually forget most of them.

It's important to explain to children what nightmares are. No one is exempt from nightmares, and they torment our children. If you remember your childhood, it's likely you woke up more than once because you were terrified by a nightmare. Young children, if nightmares haven't been explained to them, don't know if they're real or not until they're approximately seven years old.

You know immediately when your child has a nightmare. They wake up screaming, crying, scared, and in many occasions they come into your bed and don't want to sleep alone. Don't make the mistake of leaving them alone without giving them an explanation. Your children learn from you. If you don't explain it to them, they're likely to make their own judgment from whoever else they ask, or worse, they'll grow up with fears and insecurities.

Those nightmares or the dreams they have, whether they're enjoyable or not, are a reflection of what's happening around them.

If you speak and communicate with your children, you will realize the problems they have, plus their insecurities, wishes, aspirations, and fears. This way, you'll be able to help them. This is another way to maintain communication with your kids and know how to help them in this world.

How you can explain it to them:

Tell them that every being in this world dreams, whether they're human or an animal. Sometimes they won't like their dreams, but they don't have to be scared. Dreams are normal; what they dreamed isn't real and won't happen to them, your family, or anyone.

Ask them to tell you about their dream or nightmare so they can get it out of their system and can relax. Explain that if they have another bad dream, they can come to you, because you'll always be there to hear them out.

After that, turn on a night light and say a prayer (whatever religion you belong to). Wait until they fall asleep, and they'll have sweet dreams. Some children prefer to sleep with a teddy bear or stuffed animal or doll because it gives them security and companionship.

Generally, when a young child loses their mother or father, especially when they're young, this loss is reflected through dreams as desires. Dead people can appear in dreams, and this can be mysterious, especially when they appear not once but often. This happened to my mother, who lost her father when she was nine years old. Her father would appear in her dreams almost every day, to the point that her mother started to worry. She would sit down and talk to him, and her mother saw her do this on many occasions. She was becoming thinner and tired. At the time, people told her mother that her father wanted to take her away.

The truth is that no one knows why this happens. I only know that her mother prayed a lot, she took her to Church, and rebaptized her. My mother had one last dream in her childhood, in which she saw her father from across a bridge. She wanted to cross it to be with him. Beneath the bridge was her great grandmother, who took care of her as a child, who had also died. Under the bridge, there were big waves and she wore a scarf. Mother wanted to cross, and her father told her she couldn't. He was with someone else, apart from her great grandmother, someone she didn't know. According to the description, she was part of the family; however, Mother kept walking across the bridge. Her father said, "This is the last time we will see each other." My mother kept trying to cross, but her father, with a strong and authoritarian voice, told her to go back. This was not the place for her yet.

Dream: "Girl, five, who had a very enjoyable dream, wakes up telling her parents she dreamed of Santa Claus, who brought her many gifts, and talked to her."

Answer: This type of dream, in which happiness is expressed, is common in children when they don't have anything that torments them. They're simple dreams, and many times they reflect the subconscious. It's especially common during the holidays, because of what they hear, see, and desire.

Dreams that warn of coming conflicts, problems or gossip

Dream: "There was someone on a bridge and below they saw a canal. The water was murky, then they saw two crocodiles passing by. Because they saw them from above, they were only passing, but they knew the problem was coming. It was going to be two problems that were going to be solved. Because they were seeing them from above, they were seeing them from an angle from what's happening in their head." If that person solved their problem, I told them to self-analyze, to see what those two problems were. Maybe it was their work. I asked questions about their work, to understand where the problem was coming from, to help that person.

Warning dreams

Some dreams reveal messages about future problems or current ones. As you study the topic, you will learn when a dream is a warning.

Generally, I call these dreams "vaccine dreams." Just like a vaccine against the flu, it prepares you with solutions and answers. In this case, it will help you decipher a message to avoid something, so it doesn't happen to you.

Maria has a business and her dream is related to her work:

Dream: "I'm asleep and I dream that two people are coming who say they are auditors and they're coming to inspect my business.

"I got scared in the dream, because you're always scared when there's an audit; in my dream, everything was going too quickly. At the same time, I realized I might lose my business because of the way I was managing it. In the dream, I felt an internal voice tell me to save money and not spend more on unnecessary things. It also told me to open another business and get out of this one. After this I thought I woke up, but I was still asleep. I went to tell my associate they were going to audit us. Just as I was about to tell him, the auditors were already at the door."

Answer: This person came to me with an emergency that same day. I said, "This is what we call a warning dream. You're very lucky that in the dream it was clearly revealed how things would happen. At the same time, it's giving you the answer. You have to follow what the dream says. Get out of the current business, sell your shares to your associate, open another business, and look at other options. It also reflects the worry you've had about earning lots of money but not saving it. You have to change, or you'll end up on the street."

Maria called me the following week and informed me they had called her about auditing her office. They stayed in it for a week.

What does this mean? If we look at the positive, Maria's dream is one of many warning dreams that will end well. I'm glad Maria consulted it, for it will guide her and help her with the steps she must perform in her business.

Maria called me six months later. She opened a new business and closed the previous one. The auditing didn't go very well, but she came out okay in the end. She left her associate and is now saving.

Who is sending us these warning messages and why?

What would have happened if Maria had been negative? She would have said, "This is a negative dream!" and would not have taken the maximum benefit from the message. She would have gone on with her life and would have lost her business without being prepared to start another before the auditing was complete.

Fernando, a young single man, lived and worked in Colombia in a very remote and poor city in the mountains. He was the administrator of one of the estates in that region and went to work there because they paid him well. One day he had a dream that impressed him so much he changed his life.

Dream: "I'm with one of my cousins, walking toward the river. We got on a boat. That was part of our work, to transport ourselves from one place to the other, and suddenly we had an accident and died. I saw myself in my own funeral. When I was inside the coffin, it's as if my spirit woke up. The mourning shocked me so thoroughly that I woke up immediately.

"That was early in the morning before I went to work. That week, I had to get the boat to cross the river."

Fernando didn't share this dream with me at that moment because I didn't know him at the time.

He did 12 years later. Now he has a wife and two daughters and lives in Miami.

Fernando, terrified by the dream, went to work and decided to quit that same day. He told his boss he would train the person he had in mind for the position, but he would leave the same week the person was trained. He said he could no longer work in the province and would be leaving.

In what sounds like a fairy tale, that's exactly how it happened. He left that same week after training his replacement for two or three days. A week later, he received a call saying that his cousin, who also worked at the estate, and the person he had trained for his position, had taken the boat and had disappeared. There was no trace of them. They just disappeared. Today, twelve years later, he still doesn't know what happened to them.

You're likely familiar with many other cases of dreams predicting the future from your own experiences or from others. Dreams reveal many things, whether they're warnings or other messages. The key is to look for the positive and good side to them all.

*"Messages" showing a path that ends
tell you to turn back or stay put.*

If in your dreams you see one path and no others, when you get to the end of the path, you might think, "I've gotten here. Now what do I do?" That means you should realize the path has ended and wonder,

"Do I stay here, or do I go back?" You may realize it's time to go back. When you wake up, you should ask, "What does this mean?" It means that something you were doing previously was productive, but you no longer do it. It means you must go back from where you came from. You must do what you were doing before. If it was generating money, consider doing it again.

You may not like taking a step back, but sometimes it's necessary. It can be positive, like when you open a business. You start with enthusiasm and energy, but suddenly the business runs into a roadblock or doesn't go as planned. You start working less or start to care less about it. Then what? You may begin setting things aside that were once important. Perhaps at that moment you didn't have the money to pay someone, but you do today. Decisions like this come back to harm you. You must return to better ways of controlling your business.

Encouraging dreams and messages

Another type of dream is a futuristic dream. For example, you may see the sun in your dream. Here is someone else's dream I really enjoyed:

Dream: I'm looking up to the sky and I see a beautiful sun with rays coming down. The sky was covered by dark clouds, as if a storm was coming. It was a big storm, but when I looked at the sky, the sun's rays were coming down. It gave the scene a great tranquility, and I felt comfortable.

*When that person consulted with me,
I said to them:*

Lately you're going through some difficulties. Your problems will be solved, for in the difficulties you will find exits. After the storm comes the calm.

The "calm after the storm" reflects the hope you can expect after a difficulty. There will be a door to go through, and people who see this in a dream are usually going through difficulty. They will find the solution to it if they use their memory and think about how to solve the problem. That way they will find the solution to all of their complications.

Just like dreams about entering a valley and coming out, you will come out of any difficulty you're going through. If you're not in any current adversity, certain conflicts can be projected into the future. They are coming. If you are a professional, the conflict is likely to be business-related. If you're a woman it might be related to your family; if you're a man, it might be related to your work; for children, it might be related to school. It all depends on what you're dedicated to: an artist or singer, it might be related to a project you're working on. If it reflects nature, you might desire to live in nature; you may be a person who loves nature.

Messages through dreams that represent health issues for us or others around us.

The Hindu faith Chinese medicine see dreams based on the interpretation of health.

If you dream about not being able to breathe, whether it's because of strangulation, choking, or suffocation, this dream points to a respiratory problem, perhaps asthma, but can also relate to someone you see choking you in the dream.

If you feel like you're sinking in the sea and can't get out, this is a mind-related problem. The sea, the water is like our subconscious. The brain can be related to insanity or psychological problems, whether it's you or people you know.

When you have a high temperature, it's reflected through monsters and nightmares.

If in the dream you feel like you are paralyzed or can't move, it's related to your circulatory system. You don't have good circulation and you need to watch your diet and exercise more.

CHAPTER III

Darkness and Nightmares

One time someone commented to me about how they would always have nightmares in which monsters would follow them.

They asked me, "Why do I have this type of nightmare?"

My response was, "Do they bother you?"

"No, they don't bother me. They did at first, but now I'm used to always dreaming about monsters. It doesn't happen often, but every once in a while I dream of monsters that follow me."

I asked, "Do you like to watch horror movies?"

"Yes, I love watching them."

"Well! One of the reasons you might be having these nightmares is because of what you see, what your eyes capture, and what you hear."

Why did I say that? Because I saw that they were a stable person. They didn't use drugs and weren't sick. Instead, they were happy. It's rare for such a positive person like that to be having these types of dreams, the consequence of watching too many horror films. If you want to have nicer dreams, don't watch horror movies. If they don't bother you, you can keep watching that kind of film, but just know you'll have part of what you saw in your dreams.

If you're the kind of person who is scared of having nightmares, don't watch this kind of film. If you're going to watch them, do a brain washing before going to bed. Spend some time with God, or in whatever religion you practice. Ask Him to take away those bad thoughts from your mind. You'll dream beautiful things and will wake up remembering them. If you want sweet, peaceful, and positive dreams, don't continue to watch these films.

You may sometimes have nightmares if you've had some alcohol, drugs, or when we're sick. If you're a bit warm, you might have nightmares. Sometimes nightmares occur when the person has a fever. Sometimes if you eat too much before going to sleep, you can have nightmares. The same happens when you eat too little, take medication, or have pain, depending on the body part that hurts.

If you feel pain in your nightmare, one part of your body may be pressured. You might be sleeping in a bad position and your arm falls asleep. It's like an alarm.

Nightmares are expressed because of physical issues, but psychological problems can also contribute to them. Sigmund Freud's theory, that dreams are an expression of unconscious desires, shows that nightmares express a psychic conflict the dreamer wants to come to light, but the conscience interprets it as a threat to its balance.

For many cultures, like Western ones, these are just bad dreams. For others, it's a sign of problems, conflicts, or negative events that are coming. For primitive societies, they are nocturnal visits from bad spirits.

Some medications cause nightmares, such as medicines for the heart, high blood pressure, or Parkinson's disease. Without a doubt, there are many theories and many mysteries about nightmares. The truth is, you must learn to live with them and try to avoid them.

Dreams that on occasion mean death

If the dream is about tooth loss, it can point to different theories and meanings. That's why it's important to ask questions when you're interpreting a dream for another person. If someone tells me their front teeth fell out, I ask them if it hurt. It didn't hurt!

If it didn't hurt, it means it's likely not related to death. The front teeth represent close family, while the back teeth represent grandparents, and also estranged uncles, cousins, and other family members. If it does hurt, that person will hurt too. That's why it's so important to know if it hurts or not.

Since the front teeth are related to closest family, the nightmare might indicate that someone in the family might fall ill or even pass away, but not that's not always the case. It can also be related to the inferior health of the sleeper or someone very close to them who is sick. The nightmare may be telling the dreamer to watch their health and pay attention to how they are sleeping and managing their life.

Dream: "I'm in my bed and I wake up a bit frightened, because I realize my fake tooth has come out. I try to put it back in, but it hurts every time. I ended up putting it back despite the pain."

Answer: The dream is related to a family member. It seems this person is quite ill and it's probable they will pass away and their death will catch you by surprise and you'll feel it. Because the nightmare is about fake teeth, it may point to needing a root canal or a crown. If you fall and lose the tooth, if it hurts to put the tooth back in, someone in your extended family may be going through some difficulty. They may be ill.

While I don't like to touch this subject, it may be related to passing onto a better life. Some people are terrified of this subject. All humans need understand we will all pass away. Since we've been on this Earth, we all know we'll leave.

Depending on how you manage your life, you can go one way or another. That's why it's important to think and do things that seem the same but are different. You may say, "Today I would like to do, donate, help," but are you doing it? It's important to do so now. That's a part of your dreams—the realizations that result from them.

If you want to receive, you must give. Don't give as an obligation; give because you genuinely feel it. You can create a habit in your kids to give away, not throw away, and to help in their Church. They can do good deeds, and know that if someone harms them, they don't have to take revenge. Use this method of adding, subtracting, multiplying, and dividing. God is even in mathematics. If you do good things, life will go well for you. If you do something bad, what you have will become less. You will lose something. It's important to do good; if someone does you harm, and you go back to them with good, your benefit will be multiplied.

*Dream of the death of someone
but it means something else*

Dreams you dislike aren't necessarily bad. I like to give examples of what children dream because they can be useful for when your children dream. When I was a young girl, I remember having a recurring dream I didn't like very much. I didn't have it every month. It came every year or two, at a specific time.

In my dream, I saw my father dying. I never saw him dead, but I do remember seeing him dying. I was never afraid of thinking my father would die. I first had the dream when I was nine. I would see the dream as perhaps a yes, or perhaps a no. The dream repeated itself until I was eleven.

Every time I had this dream, it felt more real. I came to the conclusion it was really going to happen, so I prepared myself mentally, by thinking, "If that's what God wants, then so it shall be." The only thing I had to do was prepare myself for life. I thought, "If my father dies, what's going to happen to us?" My brothers were younger, and my mother depended on my father. At the time, she didn't work.

Starting from the age of ten or eleven, I became obsessed with learning how to make money. I wanted to convince my father to start his own business and be prepared. That way, I could make a living for myself. I just had to convince him to start a business. I would analyze what type of business it should be. When I told my mother, she didn't exactly like the idea. Maybe she thought I was too young and didn't know what I was saying. I never told my parents I kept having that dream.

Years went by and I kept going on about the same thing. I would keep having the dream. One day my father asked me, "Why do you want me to start a business?"

I replied, "Well Dad, you currently work for someone else. If you die tomorrow, what are we going to live off of if you're working to make others richer? Why don't you work for yourself and make us richer?"

Why don't we do something that can help us in the future? He told me I was right, but that's all that happened. Years went by, and when I was fourteen, I had the same dream. I told myself I had to do something. I sold ice cream and cheese. My father found the cheese for me so I could sell it from home. I also worked in the Red Cross to gain experience. In the end, my father eliminated my businesses.

My father said when children work it's because their parents can't maintain them. If you're in a stable financial position, you can say you don't need your children to work. Some are proud they can say that. I don't think that's for everyone, because the same things don't make everyone happy. I would say, I want to work when I need to work in what I like to do.

When I was young, I wanted to work to gain experience. When the moment came, I would be ready. If you see kids who don't want to work, you can help them grow and achieve their goals. The dreams and goals they might have may never come true if you don't nurture in them positivity and a strong work ethic.

CHAPTER IV

Experiences and wishes

Subconscious dreams are related to things you've lived, seen, or heard.

While I was at a dental clinic, the dental assistant shared her dream with me so I could interpret it:

Dream: "I dreamed I was in my apartment. I looked out from the balcony. From there, I could see the parking lot and I saw someone who wanted to steal my car. I immediately called the police, they came, and made a report about my stolen car."

I answered, "This type of dream seems to be from your subconscious. It could be two things: you may be involved with someone who's had an accident or they've stolen their car. Or, you're going to lose money. It could mean you're going to spend money on something, or something happened to someone."

She told me her sister had crashed and had an accident. That means it's her subconscious that is bringing messages to her mind because of what she's living, hearing, or doing. You relive your experiences in your dreams. That's why it's very important for the interpretation of dreams to know what you're going through. That can inform your interpretation. I told her she may need to help her sister, which she is doing now.

Dreams in the past, present, and future

Dreams may predict what will happen. For example, I have had dreams that have come true in ten or twenty years. Some happen the same day. As you learn to interpret them, you will realize this.

If a dream is about the past, it can help you heal past wounds, things that have happened to you or what you've lived. Reliving something that harmed you in the past can help you recover from that problem and heal the wound.

If you dream about being in your childhood home, it probably reflects a desire to be a child again, especially if you had a nice childhood or would like to go back. At the same time, dreams from the past can help your present or future.

Dreams from the present are dreams that may happen the same day, or the following week or month. As soon as you wake up, you know you had an intense dream.

Example: In my dream, I went into a closed space where some children were. I saw a person who had skin that seemed transparent, like an onion peel, and their veins were visible, as if they were deformed. I woke up with a horrible feeling; the children who were with that person had the deformity and two others were bearded twins.

When I woke up, I realized those dreams with deformities seem to point to an illness. I realized something might be going to happen to me. Maybe one of my kids was going to fall ill. I was sure it was nothing serious, but it might be something upsetting. When I woke up, I had chills and the air conditioning was making my skin cold. Then I felt warm, as if I had a bit of the flu. That's when I realized I was getting sick.

When we learn to identify our dreams and realize they're reflecting something in the present, a dream that seems horrifying becomes very simple. In fact, I went that same day to the doctor. I had a bit of a cough, a little bit of a cold, and nothing to worry about.

Dream that reflects financial improvement

Here's a dream from a woman who was losing her house and going through a financial crisis. She was at a point of almost losing her property. What happened?

Cora had this dream: "I saw a big tree, beautiful and well nurtured, with many beautiful fruits. They were different types of fruit and I don't remember what kind, only that the tree was full of fruit."

So then what? I said to her, "You're going through something in which improvement is very visible."

She told me she was losing her home.

I answered: "Don't worry, you're not going to lose your house. You're going to get it back. You're going to have a change in your life and you'll earn money." I asked what she did, and if she had any projects in mind.

She told me she wanted to set up an atelier (a workshop or studio, especially one used by an artist or designer).

I said to her: "Keep going, you're going to be able to do it and it will go well. In fact, I feel like that will pay off your house.

Almost a year later, I saw her again and she told me, "What you said to me was true. I opened my atelier and it started with only me sewing, but then I hired a pattern maker. I found people who sold me fabrics, and now I make pants and women's underwear. It's going well for me, and I didn't lose my house."

If you fly, land, and fly again and land, it's because you are in short- and long-term projects. You have several projects and you can't decide which one to focus on. If you tackle just one at a time, it will work better. Landing means you're going down, but it doesn't mean anything bad. You're only landing, not harming yourself.

If you fall without harming yourself, the most likely meaning is that you'll have minor losses and small conflicts, but you'll come out okay. You'll know how to handle each situation and confront the obstacles. Planes are some of the strongest machines, with the ability to maintain themselves in the air. That means your projects are big and that is how you reflect them. If the plane falls and crashes, that's how your ideas will be handled. That's why it's important to go back, reflect on yourself and what your weak points are, what you aren't doing and what you want to do. That way you reinforce what you're weak in and can avoid a problem. Sometimes a plane crash reflects your subconscious. If you heard something in the news related to a plane crash, you may dream about it.

If you're preparing to travel and have that inner fear, it's your subconscious. It's projected in that way. If in the dream you land safely, that's how it will be. This is how the dream influences our life. Ships and planes may appear at a certain point. If it's a big ship, it points to changes related to seasons, such as moving, changing careers or workplaces, or even moving to a new country. It may even point to a change in ourselves.

Dream: "Someone was driving a machine that was like a car, but was going the opposite way. After trying to take it in the other direction, it took too long and lost a lot of time."

When that person woke up, they called me and told me about their dream. I told them, "This is a dream about the present, possibly even today. Maybe you'll be wandering the streets because you forgot something, because you went back."

He called me again and told me I was right. He had gone out without his credit card and his wallet, and had to go to his office, then his house, and subsequently found his items.

Your Dreams and You

Dreams with money

A friend called me and told me about his dream: he saw his sister getting really thin, and in the dream his sister was giving him ten cents.

Answer: "It's likely you have financial issues, but you will always be helping your sister with her problems."

He replied and said yes, then I said: "You're going to send her less money than you're used to. If you send her the same amount, you'll have financial difficulties. Don't send the same amount. There also could be some family health issues."

He came back to me with the same dream, except this time she wasn't thin; she was better. Instead of giving him ten cents she gave him a dollar. When he consulted me again, I said, "That means you've been going through financial difficulty like I told you. Now your problems are starting to see the light and starting to get on a better path. Your finances are getting better, and you'll start sending her more money."

He told me I was right, that he had some money issues and a really big crisis, but now it seems things are getting better.

He had a third and last dream, at least from what I know. He told me he saw his sister well, not thin. This time, she gave him a ten dollar bill. He consulted me again.

I said, "Well your situation hasn't improved completely, but it's better than it was before."

In fact, he told me his situation had improved.

In your dreams, take every factor into account. In this case, the quantity of money the sister gave her brother in the dream was important.

CHAPTER V

Fantasies, sex, romance, kisses in dreams

Romantic dreams, whether they depict kisses or other physical acts like holding hands, show us how to love.

It doesn't matter if you're young without any sexual experience, or older. It's likely you've dreamed about these types of physical affection more than once, with people you know, strangers, people you like or are in love with, and people who aren't your type at all, even of your same sex.

Don't be afraid when I say same sex. Having relations in your dream with someone of the same sex doesn't mean you're homosexual. It represents that this person has something you admire or want.

Kisses are a good sign, if you receive them, and more if the person who gives them to you has a good relationship with you. If you don't get any kisses, it's not a good sign. If the kiss is on your forehead, it's a sign of friendship; if it's on your cheek, it indicates possible improvement.

People who have an active sex life have these types of sexual dreams, as do people who are single. It's a healthy way of maintaining the reproductive organs. The brain sends messages to every part of the body, to check if the system is functioning or not, through what you see and do in your dreams.

These dreams have a vital function and can be very positive to the dreamer when they're awake. Dreams help in reaching complete satisfaction and reinforce the capacity of our reproduction; therefore, it helps in the reproduction of our species.

Romantic dreams that don't result in the sexual act, but include kisses, hugs, and lots of love, can demonstrate the desires of the dreamer. These dreams are generally more common in women; women tend to be more romantic and want to receive more affection. If you have these types of dreams, it's possible you're not getting enough romanticism from your partner.

You may have romantic dreams with public figures such as politicians, artists, or singers, because of what you see, hear, or read. If you want to dream about someone, about 90% of the time, you won't dream about them when you want to. Instead, when you think about them the least, that's when it's most likely you will dream about them.

Dream about an artist

I dreamed about being on a stage or balcony and I would see a couple artists pass by. One of them was Ben Affleck. He's been in my dreams twice! It's funny, but it doesn't necessarily mean I have an obsession with him. I'm not the kind of person who is obsessed about actors, but dreaming about celebrities can mean many things.

If you dream about a celebrity, you may admire something about that person. Perhaps, if you dream about an artist, you may be interested in artistic things. Maybe you will have a new job soon. Maybe what you are currently doing is a bit boring, and you want to put a bit of happiness and enjoyment into our lives.

In my case (feel free to form your own opinion), I saw the actor Ben Affleck. He was walking, and I said hello, but I didn't go near him. Other celebrities, artists, and singers were there. I got involved with one and kissed him on the cheek. One them was sort of interested in me.

If you're married and kiss someone else in your dream, it doesn't mean you're being unfaithful, or want to be unfaithful. Kisses are simply messages. A kiss can also mean something different depending on to whom the kiss is given. In this case, it was a kiss to a stranger from television or the music industry.

If you or the person didn't feel anything in your dream, it may indicate fear and confusion.

Infidelity in dreams

Don't feel bad when you have these kinds of dreams. They're very common in both happily married and less satisfying relationships. You're not the only who's had this dream. Generally, infidelity in dreams reflects having a long marital life, as long as it's not your subconscious that's living it. In other words, if your partner hasn't done anything to make you think about infidelity, don't worry.

On some occasions, these dreams indicate a fear that you have. Perhaps you are a jealous person, or you don't want to lose that person. If you have this kind of dream and it ends up being true, it will only a passing thing. Your partner still loves you. In dreams, when infidelities happen and they are true, it's a warning dream and a vaccine at the same time so you're prepared for what's coming.

Think about what you will do if you discover it's true. It might be something that is passing and your partner loves you. If that's the case, you're having this dream so you can fight for and protect your home.

It's also possible these dreams reflect that the partner who commits adultery is attracted to another person, because their partner, in this case the dreamer, isn't dedicating enough to them. The relationship has become monotonous, and they need a bit of romance. They could go on vacation without the kids or to go somewhere private, just the two of them.

Dreams related to adultery can point to problems for the couple but could also be linked to the creative activities of the dreamer. Having these dreams doesn't mean you're in a bad place. Some couples who are happily married repeatedly keep having these dreams.

Seeing your rival

If you see your rival in your dream, it's very important to decipher it. It has a message that will help you know how that person thinks and how you can benefit from the dream. Take advantage of it. Try to understand why that person may not like you, if they want to harm you, how they act, or what they're going to do. The dream can reveal how they think and how to read their mind. It can decipher enigmas regarding your own relationship. At the same time, you can find out that the person is yourself, something you envy or want from them, or that they envy you. Reflect on this type of dream and ask questions to confront what this person wants. In the same dream, you can read their mind and feelings, and why they're in your dreams. Remember this dream represents obstacles; if you beat your rival in your dream, you'll come out okay.

Dictionary of dreams and their lucky number

Letter A

Abandonment: Not a very fortunate dream, indicates loss of some projects you had in mind. Whether you have been abandoned or you have abandoned someone, you will have conflicts. LN*12154, (4)

Accessories: If they are given to you and you accept, it's a bad sign. If you decline them, it's a good sign. If you receive them, but don't use them, that means good times after some time. LN*13355, (8)

Accident: Dreams related to accidents are warnings. We must pay more attention to what we are doing. The same dream doesn't mean the same thing for different people. It reveals stress; we generally have these dreams when we are involved in some important matter. Accidents at sea are related to love. Accidents in the air are related to projects not yet accomplished that will fall down. Car accidents and others, mean loss of money. LN*13397, (5)

Accusation: Depends on the magnitude of the dream. It is related to work or legal problems. Do not involve yourself in anything that will take away your tranquility. It is recommended that you go over things more than once. LN*13336, (7)

Actors: You are being a bit superficial; if you are the actor or actress, this represents triumph. LN*13261, (4)

Abdomen: If you see yourself with a bountiful abdomen, it is abundance; if it is scrawny, this means financial difficulties. LN*12465, (9)

Abortion: Related to the health of your partner and their mood and frame of mind. LN*12694, (4)

Abundance: Seeing yourself in abundance is good if you wake up happy. This means you'll have more. If you are a wealthy person and you wake up sad, the dream shows you are afraid of losing your wealth, and you will have difficulties in your finance. If you are not wealthy, it is always a fortunate message for your financial side. LN*12359, (2)

Abuse: If someone abuses you, it is a warning dream and it is important to reflect on it, especially if you know the abuser. If it is you who abuses yourself, you will have success after much effort. LN*12315, (3)

Abscess: If you are sick, you will recover quickly; if not, you will purify yourself of events in your life. LN*12137, (5)

Abstinence: If it is from alcohol or dreams, it's short term good fortune. LN*12125, (11)

Abyss: Seeing it in dreams is a sign of difficulties. The larger it is and the more fear it causes, the bigger is the problem; if you don't fall into the abyss, you'll resolve your complications; if you do, you will have difficulties. Don't lend money right now because it will not be given back. If you think about expanding your business, wait until the storm has passed. LN*12711, (3)

Advance: You know how to take advantage of the right moment and are very ambitious. LN*14414, (5)

Admiration: It's good to be admired or to be the admirer. You are a good friend and have good friends, but if you wake up feeling afflicted, it means the contrary. LN*14495, (5)

Adultery: It is a good sign and good morality. If you feel uncomfortable in the dream, this means the contrary. LN*14335, (7)

Affection: If affection really exists, you may receive an inheritance. If affection does not exist, or if you don't know, it is the contrary. Affection amongst children means high earnings. LN*16657, (7)

Africa: You will make new friendships, and you desire to meet new people. LN*16994, (2)

Aging: If it worries you, it is a sign of illness. If you are satisfied with the image of being older, it means wisdom. LN*17593, (7)

Agitated: Sign of culmination of a project not yet completed. LN*17923, (4)

Agony: A warning of obstacles, especially common in obsessive workers. LN*17657, (8)

Agriculture: Everything related to agriculture, such as nature, growth, and giving life, means long lasting happiness. LN*17991, (9)

Air: If it's nice, calm and clear, your goals will be achieved. If it's a strong air current, take precautions with important decisions. Do not take any precipitated measures until your head is clear. LN*199, (1)

Album: If you see photos, it means a possible end of an era and a start of another. If you wake up melancholic or see yourself sad, it means memories. LN*13234, (4)

Alley: The more narrow the alley, the fewer exits you have. The best thing to do is go back out from where you came and not go into it. There are difficult conflicts to resolve. If the alley is dark and without exits, recovery will be difficult for you. If you go in and find an exit, you will come out okay from everything. LN*13357, (1)

Almond: If you see the almond flower, it's a good sign. If the flower falls to the ground, it's not a good sign. Think about what first comes to mind that might be falling or about to fall in your life. LN*13469, (6)

Altar: It's not always fortunate and depends on who is at the altar. If it's you, it's not a fortunate dream, unless you are close to getting married. If it's a stranger, it doesn't have much importance, but if you know the person, it means they will start a serious relationship. LN*13219, (7)

Amber: Small profits. LN*14259, (21)

Ambition: If it is measured ambition, this is positive in your business; if it is exaggerated, the contrary. LN*14294, (2)

Amulet: If you have one, it means you are about to make important life decisions. It's necessary to you reevaluate the decision you are about to take. The answer is within yourself and not the amulet. If it is gifted to you, don't trust it too easily. LN*14337, (9)

Ancestors: Since they are no longer with us, generally they reappear to reveal enigmas or solutions. If you are not behaving well, they will reappear so you can explain your behavior. If you don't change, they will come back. LN*15351, (6)

Anchor: If it is buried in the sea, you will be stalled for a while. If you see they are wheeling it in to take off, you will have positive changes in your life. LN*15386, (5)

Angel: It is always good to dream about angels, whether they are one or various. Having good relationships with them is better. Good times are coming. LN*15753, (21)

Animals: Depends if the animal is fat, scrawny, sick, or in good condition. For the best interpretation, go by the animal. Fish swimming freely means fortune. If the animals are in the position to attack, someone wants to harm you. The contrary if they are docile. Reptiles represent gossip and conflict; birds are the symbol of strength to achieve goals if we see them in good condition and flying. The color of the animal is also important. LN*36545, (5)

Ants: Depends on the type of ant. If they're crazy ants, you're without direction. If they're outside, it's productive business activity. In your home, possible illness of you or a family member. LN*1521, (9)

Antipathy: If you feel bad being unfriendly to others, this is a bad sign. If you like it, then this is good. LN*15299, (8)

Anvil: Prosperity and work for consecutiveness and patience. If they're not noisy, abnegation. LN*15493, (4)

Appetite: Deficiencies, whether in health or other aspects. Points to deficiencies if you eat too much as well. Moderately, this means good in finances. LN*17759, (2)

Applause: If they clap for you, it's hypocrisy. If you're looking for the approval of others when you should only look for your own. If instead in your life you are an artist, this doesn't count; it's simply your subconscious. If you are applauding, you are being a bit envious. LN*17731, (1)

Apple: Red apples mean prosperity. Green and acid apples mean immaturity and gains at the same time. If you are a professional, it reflects your business. If you are a housewife, improvement in your home and finances. Just like the apple is what made Eve sin, it represents the desire to commit adultery. LN*17735, (5)

Archive: Related to work, you wish for a better change. If you look in the archive, you will find what you're looking for. LN*19389, (3)

Artist: We admire or wish to be anything like an artist professionally; if your head is up, you will be on a stage, in an artistic way, a new life path, changes in your work. It also means flattery. LN*19293, (6)

Art Gallery: Abundance and prestige. LN*19278, (9)

Assassination: Avoid risks for some time at all costs. If you take them, make sure someone with experience gives their input, such as a lawyer if it is related to legal matters. LN*11113, (7)

Astrologist: If you consult or read about the topic, you are looking for an answer to something. If you are the astrologist, you are looking to improve yourself in your knowledge. LN*11297, (2)

Attacking: If you are attacked, it indicates possible annoyances. If you're the attacker, you'll be fine after a problem. LN*12218, (5)

Autograph: Start of new projects, change of life. LN*13265, (8)

Avocado: If the avocado is in good condition, you will be valued by your close relatives and friends; it means the opposite if it's rotten. LN*14632, (7)

Axe: Everything that has to do with cold steel represents the coming of struggles. LN*165, (3)

Letter B

Baby: It's bad luck if you see a defenseless baby who can't fend for itself. You will have some complications but they will be resolved. If the baby is sick, there might be someone in serious condition in your family. On the contrary, if the child is a little bit older and robust, this is good luck. LN*2127, (3)

Bacchanalia: If you party a lot, be careful of excesses such as alcohol. If you don't party, you need to have fun. Excesses are the problem. LN*21335, (5)

Ball: Triumph through discipline and persistence. LN*2133, (9)

Bald: If a man is genetically bald from his family, it's a sign he will begin to lose hair. LN*2134, (1)

Bald spot: If as a woman, you have a bald spot, this means finding a partner will be difficult. Any loss of hair is sign of loss of money or health. LN*21347, (8)

Bankruptcy: Analyze all your projects, especially those that require an investment, for it may leave you in misery. Be very cautious and ask for professional advice. LN*21524, (5)

Bar: be prudent with everything, especially if you see yourself drinking too much. LN*219, (3)

Barefaced: Loss of character, money, or immaturity, depending on the situation. If you appear as a child or a man without a mustache or beard if you usually have one and appear without it, it will be in your work. LN*21951, (9)

Barefoot: Related to hard work and difficulties that you will resolve only with perseverance. If you see yourself walking barefoot on a rocky path, you have a long way to go before getting where you want. Have patience and don't give up. LN*21952, (1)

Bats: If they scare you, insecurity, and the possible start of depression. Take care of your mood, and don't let anything or anyone lower your self-esteem. If you feel good, new positive and adventurous phase of your life. LN*2121, (6)

Bathing: Outdoors, it's a good sign; it indicates liberty. If you are in a closed bathroom, it indicates conflicts. You are looking at things too narrow-mindedly. LN*21283, (7)

Beans: Means having good health, whether you're eating them or cooking them. Collecting them or seeing them points to gains. LN*25151, (5)

Bear: If the bear attacks you and you win, you'll come out victorious. If you don't, you'll face adversities. LN*2519, (8)

Beard: Speaks to resolution of conflict. A white beard means you will resolve a problem wisely. LN*25194, (21)

Beauty salon: It's not the best thing to see yourself in a beauty salon. If they're cutting your hair, it indicates possible material losses. If you're the hairdresser, it's a good sign and indicates prosperity. LN*25139, (2)

Bedroom: If it is several bedrooms, things will go well in the moment you least expect it. One room, you have secrets to uncover. If it is empty, someone wants to abandon you or you will quit a job, project, or relationship. Dirty or messy room indicates illness of the dreamer. If it is a family member's room, illness of the family member. LN*25497, (9)

Belt buckle: If it's in good state, this is good luck. If it's damaged or comes off, it's a warning of difficulties. LN*25329, (21)

Bees: This is a good sign in any matter, and more so in matters of money, property, and improvement for those who have it. If they sting you, you will have some difficulties. If you kill the bees, you will have improvement. LN*2551, (4)

Beetroot: Related to various factors, you have to ask yourself. Does it pertain to your health or ideals? If health, take care of yourself. If ideals, you're loyal to your ideas and need to be clear that life is a gift. LN*25525, (1)

Beggar: If you see a beggar, the social state of your country worries you. If you are helping them, you are interested in something to do with philanthropy. LN*25771, (4)

Begging: You've let some parts of yourself go, not only your exterior but also your interior. Be careful and value yourself. If you're dirty and broken, it relates to problems with letting go of your health. LN*25773, (6)

Bible: Happiness, triumphs.

Bicycle: If you are an adult and don't use a bike but you see yourself on it, this means you will soon have to make important decisions. If you see yourself as a child, it indicates fond memories and perhaps you will visit someone you haven't seen in decades. LN*29372, (5)

Bill/Invoice: Giving it to someone who owes you, fear on losing investments. Paying it, good luck and fortune. Not paying it, people are talking about you. LN*2933, (8)

Birth: The start of everything in life. You're in a new project. It indicates abundance if you're married. If you see yourself as a single mom, you'll go through problems. If you're happy being a single mom you'll do well. LN*29928, (3)

Bittersweet taste: Indicates contradictions. Relationships with toxic tendencies. Reevaluate romantic connections and relationships with your close relatives. LN*29227, (4)

Blind: If you see yourself blind, you are in a relationship in which you don't want to see your own faults. You love that person a lot. If eyesight recovery, your veil has fallen for the person you love. LN*23954, (5)

Blueprints: You have the character of a leader or are working towards it. If you see prints of forests or calculations, you have everything under control. If you see prints to a treasure, you're in or want to be in a project difficult to fulfill. LN*23356, (1)

Blood: The interpretation depends on how the dream progresses. What does blood represent for you? If you're scared, it's a negative result in your health and mood. Positive, it's good in various aspects including love. LN*23664, (3)

Boar: If you are chased by this animal or come out injured, you've encountered a dangerous enemy. If you kill it, you will be victorious. LN*2619, (9)

Boat/Ship: Changes in your life. If you are alone, the change will only involve yourself and you don't want to involve anyone else. If you fall from the boat, your love issues will be resolved if you float up to the surface. If the sea is agitated, you are experiencing rampant passions. LN*2612, (11)

Bodyguard: Instinct of overprotection of your loved ones. LN*26476, (7)

Bomb: If it is a water bomb and the water is clean, it's prosperity and blessings. Dirty water indicates difficulties. If you are in a bombardment and you hear it end, you will come out unharmed from a problem and you will start a new phase of your life. Hearing a bomb means problems. LN*2642, (5)

Boss: It depends on the current relationship you have with your boss. Usually indicates delicate situations with your job that have nothing to do with love. LN*2611, (1)

Bottle: If it is empty, bad luck in love. If filled with clear liquid, good health and wellbeing. Hot liquid or dark, indicates troubles in your health. Check yourself periodically. LN*26228, (2)

Box: An empty box means your plans will come out backwards. Finding something in the box is good luck. LN*266, (5)

Breast-feed: Maternal instinct. You wish to be a mother if you haven't yet, or you want to have another baby. Maybe you are being too maternal with your partner. Recommendation: your partner doesn't want his mother in the bedroom. LN*29515, (4)

- If your children are adults, this dream indicates you want to be closer to your children. If they are still babies, this means sweetness, tenderness, and love, combined with your subconscious for what you do. If you did not breastfeed, feeling of guilt, and if you did, nice memories.

Branch: Everything that has to do with trees, nature, and growth in what your interests are focused in at the moment. LN*29152, (1)

Breaking a glass: If it had ice in it, represents the death of a family member. It also represents the health of those you love most. LN*29517, (6)

Bricks: Broken, your plans are being threatened. If someone breaks your bricks, problems at home or related to a work project. Building with bricks indicate solid bases, whether you work in this dream or your dreams are telling you to do the work. LN*29933, (8)

Bridge: It's a step to other ways or new events. It's a positive sign if you cross it. If you don't cross it, take away your fear and lack of self-confidence. LN*29943, (9)

Brush: If it's a paintbrush, you are in an artistic moment. Take advantage of it. LN*29318, (5)

Bubbles: Disappointment. If children are playing with the bubbles, it means the opposite. LN*23229. (9)

Building: Fulfilling aspirations. The higher the building, the higher your benefit. LN*23937, (6)

Bull: For men, it's related to virility, potency, and daring. For women, love adventures. LN*2333, (2)

Burning yourself: It's a dream with an opposite meaning; it's related to new and good relations. Possible positive change. LN*23953, (4)

Butterfly: Good news, it indicates a metamorphosis, whether it's in you or someone else, depending on the dream. If you see them in the daytime, it's a good sign, especially if they are colorful and bright. LN*23223, (9)

Letter C

Cabaret: Desire to distract yourself. LN*31217, (5)

Cage: Generally interpreted as negative, for it's prison. If we see ourselves encaged, all our expectations and dreams are repressed. Free yourself. A wild encaged animal, triumph. Lack of freedom of speech. LN*3175, (7)

Cane: Possible illness or difficulty. LN*3155, (5)

Carpet: Good sign if you are in the right place. If it's the wrong place, you'll have to go the extra mile to achieve your goals. If it burns, it will warn you against gossip. Buying carpets, you will discover something in your favor. Installing them, a bad sign. LN*31977, (9)

Cactus: Pay more attention to the steps you take to avoid problems. LN*31324, (4)

Canals: If they are very narrow and the water is dark and dirty, conflicts await. If they are wide and the water is clear, you will resolve any problem or project you stumble upon. LN*31514, (5)

Cajolery: Fake friends. LN*31166, (8)

Car: Cars represent the risks you take. When you are drinking, this symbolizes your life, for you are putting it at risk. Also indicates the desire to have that car, depending on who dreams. Crashing is loss of money, funeral car. Beware of any traps, problems, and don't make any bets. It's important to pay attention to everything. Don't trust the generosity of people you think love you too much. LN*319, (4)

- If it is a child driving the car, this is common. These are desires. The child wants to do the same as the parent. Maybe this will be a child who likes racecars.

Cards: Uncontrolled. LN*31941, (9)

Cat: Femininity, intuition, magic. The color of the cat can alter the meaning of the dream. LN*312, (6)

Carrot: If you have it in your right hand, you'll be okay from any problem. Eating it, inheritance. LN*31998, (3)

Cast/plaster: You've been a bit hyperactive and need to be more rested. If the cast is white, you'll come out okay from the problems you're in. Cast on the foot, need to meditate. LN*3112, (7)

Cattle/Livestock: The cow is good luck in finance. If the cattle are nice, you will have long lasting money. If they're not, you will have a year of financial difficulties. LN*31228, (7)

Cement: A present, job offer, or money awaits. LN*35456, (5)

Chains: If you are tied, your problems have been with you for a while. Visualize yourself breaking free from them so you can be liberated of those ties you have with your past that don't allow you to move forward. If you break them in the dream, you will finally be free of a long-lasting problem. LN*38196, (9)

Charity/Charitable: Giving in dreams assures unexpected wealth. Receiving means you're mentally limiting yourself. LN*38199, (3)

Chess: Calculated, patient, and intelligent. I recommend you learn how to play it because if you dreamt it, it's for a reason. Something positive will happen. LN*38511, (9)

Cheering: Fake friends. LN*38553, (6)

Cheese: Good or bad, depending on the cheese. If it's sweet, it's good. Bitter or damaged cheese, shows worries about non analyzed actions. LN*385515, (9)

Children: When you dream about your son, it refers to your daughter, and vice versa. Generally if you dream about your kids and they are adults but you see them as babies, it's because you've lost them over time and want to make up for lost time, if you have a good relationship with them. If you don't, it's to see how you've failed and repair it. It's of very good luck to see them in good state and health. If they are sick, conflicts. If you see them happy and playing, it's family improvement. If the child is small and doesn't know how to walk and is trying to make its first steps and falls trying to walk, you're in a difficult project. LN*38935, (1)

Infant/Kids: LN*95617, (4)

Christmas: Happiness and union in the family. Many lights and Christmas tree, growth, improvement. LN*38999, (11)

Choking: For business this is bad news, but if you save yourself or are saved, you'll be okay. If you have respiratory problems or are sick, pay no attention to this dream. LN*38623, (4)

Church: Different meanings, such as honor, regret, bliss, concealment, and happiness. If you see yourself praying, good times. If you are fighting in the office, misery. For single people, possible commitment. LN*38392, (5)

Climbing: If you are climbing a mountain and reach the finish line, this is success in whatever you put your mind to. If you fall, your goals are higher than your capabilities. If you come out unharmed, you will reach the finish with difficulties. LN*33945, (6)

Clouds: Internal peace, reflecting a dreamer who dreams when awake. Shows a projection towards your future, the way you will reach your objective, even if sometimes you must come down to Earth. LN*33635, (2)

Clover: Good in every aspect. Check that you're using more time off in your life. LN*33645, (21)

Coat: If you see yourself in dreams with too much clothing on, it's not a good thing. Less clothing is better. On the other hand, if you buy a coat it's good, and the opposite is true if you're taking it off. LN*3612, (3)

Coffee: Seeing yourself grinding the coffee means strength of character. Coffee beans, fortune and intellect. If the coffee spills, setbacks. LN*36661, (4)

Coffin: Annoyances of every kind. Avoid conflicts at all cost. LN*36665, (8)

Color blue: Light blue like the sky represents peace and purity. Dark blue, strength and dominion. Blue is the color of improvement and prosperity. LN*36364, (4)

Color black: As a color, it is the dark part and negative side of us. As the mystical part, it's power. LN*23132, (2)

Color green: Color of nature. Pine green, evil, threat; light green, proximity of money, wealth. LN*79555, (4)

Color grey: It refers to the sky, coming problems. If it is the color itself it's the combination of black and white and it will always go over to the light color, positivity, and improvement. It will all depend on your mood, and that will be what determines the meaning. If it's to the dark, conflicts in your mood and passing depressions. LN*7957, (1)

Color red: Dominant color, deep love. If it's light, it's affection towards someone. Dark, violence, strong temper, and violent passions. LN*954, (9)

Color pink: Love for our children, family, stability and calm. LN*7952, (5)

Column: Represents stability. Four columns, complete stability representing God, you, your family, and career. Two, stability in love. LN*36339, (6)

Complaints: Negativity, could be with negative people or you are being negative. LN*36473, (5)

Composing: You don't contemplate failure. You have high self-esteem. Good times are coming. Take advantage of this phase of your life. LN*36471, (21)

Construction: Whether it's a building or a house, the bigger the construction, the bigger your expectations and possibilities will be. LN*36511, (7)

Cookies/Biscuits: Insufficiencies. Biscuits with fruit, the meaning depends on what the fruit means. Grape biscuits, expansion of your gains. Combined with sweets or chocolate, you will receive a present. LN*36626, (5)

Cow: Dreaming about them while they're fat and beautiful, prosperity, better times will come. The opposite, loss of money, misery. LN*365, (5)

Crack: Everything that has to do with breaking, whether it's your body or an object, predicts problems of every kind. Check what broke in the dream and examine the object now that it's a composed meaning. Example: furniture cracking is arguments at home. LN*39132, (9)

Your Dreams and You

Cricket: Listening to it, prosperity, happy days, better times. If you can't hear it, necessity to improve. LN*39939, (6)

Crocodiles/Alligators: Animals that crawl are problems. They indicate gossip or conflicts among people. If you confront them or you see them pass, the problem will go away. LN*39631, (4)

Cotton: Exquisite and good times. LN*36222, (6)

Cottage: Related to love depending, on the circumstances and events. In a cottage with your friends, rifts in love. Only looking at the cottage means a person that attracts you will be closer. LN*36224, (8)

Crying: Depends on the situation. If you're crying because of mishaps or drastic changes in your life, you'll have big complications. If it's not because of mishaps, the contrary. LN*39793, (4)

Crashing: Possible loss of money. This can also be a warning dream. Check your car and take it to the mechanic. You can avoid a catastrophe your angels are warning you about through the dream. LN*39112, (7)

Crawling: Bad sign in love life matters. Find your place and reflect about how much you are giving. Analyze if the relationship is reciprocal. LN*39156, (6)

Crystal: When there are crystal walls through which you see yourself, this is a very fortunate dream. If you are seeking clarity in which you want to project yourself, where you want to go, and how you see yourself. For business people this is good, because it means your efforts are going to be fruitful. A housewife who is seeing the results of her labor, her children are doing well in school, and her spousal relationship is going well. Young person, things are looking good. At work everything is clear, and there are no conflicts. LN*39716, (9)

Cup: If it's empty, lots of debt and a lot of projects and indecision. It's good sign if the cup is clean. If it's glass and you see clear water, you're making good decisions. If the cup and the water are dirty, illness. If an ill person dreams this, possible death of the dreamer. LN*337, (4)

Curls: If you have straight hair and appear with curly hair, desire to be rebellious. If you have curly hair, this dream means nothing. LN*33931, (1)

Cyst: Worries. LN*3712, (4)

Letter D

Dagger: Be careful exposing yourself to fights. Everything that has to do with blades are fights. If you don't cut yourself, it's only a warning. If you do, you have to control your impulsive temper. LN*41775, (6)

Dancing: It's fortunate to see yourself dancing in your own house. A costume dance, beware of lies and stop being so fake. Dancing with a woman means fear of the opposite sex. Dancing between men, the fear of falling in love with another man. LN*41533, (7)

Darkness: We are not sure of what we want, or they see us this way. Conflicts are coming. LN*41923, (6)

Darn: New and good friendships. Putting on darned clothing, your financial woes will worsen. Gossip. LN*4195, (9)

Dawn: Seeing the dawn means quick achievement of your goals. Sunset means it will take longer, but with hard work and perseverance you will achieve anything. Recommendation: if you experience sunset, organizing yourself will make things easier and will take you to the root of the problem. LN*4155, (6)

Death: Burying or finishing a part of your life and starting a new one. LN*45128, (2)

Deformations: Seeing any kind of deformation in dreams, whether in people or animals, isn't good luck. Be careful with appearances and do not get into legal issues. LN*45661, (4)

Dejection: Extreme decay and weakness. LN*45157, (4)

Dentist: Associated with health, for teeth represent your health and your family's. Son or daughter at the dentist, health problem related to one of your kids. LN*45523, (1)

Destroying: If someone destroys something that belongs to you, your enemies envy you because you are in a good place. If it is the opposite, it is you who destroys. Self-analyze yourself to see what part of yourself you are destroying. LN*45127, (1)

Diamond: Depending on the financial status of the dreamer, it can have different interpretations. It can be seen as negative or positive. For a woman, possible commitment or marriage. For others, it is an excellent sign of financial gains. LN*49146, (6)

Dice: You are letting yourself go by luck and events without stopping to analyze what is best for you. LN*4935, (21)

Dirt/Filth: Feeling of guilt if you see yourself filthy or possibly sick. If it's another person who's filthy, conflicts await. Washing dirty clothing, you'll try to resolve the problem. LN*49921, (7)

Disobedience: Disagreements with family members. Analyze the event, and from whom this disobedience comes. If it's you, desire for freedom. If it's your children, fear. LN*49162, (4)

Disabled: Warning of obstacles. If you recover, you'll come out of the situation. LN*49119, (6)

Ditch: Represents obstacles. Falling into a ditch means problems. Coming out unharmed, you'll get better soon. Being in one or seeing one, but not falling in, options and possibilities. If you are digging the dich, you're about to discover a secret. LN*49238, (8)

Dragon: Happiness and fortune. If it wants to attack you with fire, disappointment in love. LN*49172, (5)

Drink: If it is clear and fresh, this means success. Dirty, problems. LN*49952, (2)

Drinking water: You'll get engaged. If the water is clean, you'll be happy. If the water is dirty, you'll suffer. LN*49953, (3)

Driving: Without a destination, you don't know where you're going, loss of time. Projects that aren't giving you much, you're losing perspective. You're going to have a time in your life when you don't know which direction to take. LN*49943, (11)

Drum: Changes in your favor. LN*4934, (2)

Dog: The dog can represent a loved one. It also represents that someone isn't being loyal to you. LN*467, (8)

Dough: Get used to changes. If you're making the dough, get your mind creative, inventive, and put it to work, you'll triumph. Finding bumps in the dough while you make it, you will have adversity, but keep going. They're only passing. LN*46378, (1)

Dungeon: Take care of your health because an illness awaits. If there is someone you know in prison, this doesn't apply to you. LN*43577, (21)

Dusk: Minor problems without big repercussions. LN*4312, (1)

Dwarf: Family conflicts. LN*45196, (7)

Letter E

Eagle: If you identify yourself with the eagle, it represents success in your matters. If it attacks you, difficulties. Dead or injured, financial losses. Where it flies is important. Upwards, that will be your success; downwards, difficulties. From east to west, you will reach your goal more quickly; from west to east, it will take longer. LN*51735, (3)

Ears: This is more for women because we are more additive. Related to the sensual and our desires. If we show our ears, we want to be seen. LN*5191, (7)

Eating: If you see yourself eating too much, this is a problem regarding your health. Eating with a loved one, friends or family, good relationships. Eating alone is sadness that torments you. LN*51293, (2)

Elephant: If you see it healthy and free, good fortune, new and important friendships, noble friends and freedom. If the elephant is in a cage, danger. LN*53577, (9)

Elevator: Going up is good luck, represents an increase in salary, position, wealth; if you are going down, misery. If you see yourself trapped, frustration with a project or in a particular person. An elevator with friends and family, good relations and a negotiation with an associate. LN*53549, (8)

Elevator/lift: Just like a staircase, if the elevator goes up this is good fortune, possible promotion, and success. The contrary if going down. LN*53549, (8)

Elevating/elevation: Every elevation is positive in any aspect of your life. Reaching somewhere higher, fulfilling your goals. If your body is being elevated, spirituality. LN*53546, (5)

Emerald: If you buy it, well being; using it, financial bitterness. Very ostentatious jewelry, if you have money, is not a good sign, but if you are poor, it shows your sign to overcome this. If it is a green rock, it foretells hard work with financial reward. For the poor, easily; for the rich, with difficulty. Middle-class people will find labor through work. LN*54598, (4)

Emperor/Empress: If you see them in a distance, desire to overcome. If you are one, realization. LN*54756, (9)

Employee: If you see yourself in the dream in your same job, your job is absorbing you. Take a mini vacation or relax when you get home. If you get a promotion, desire of realization that you are doing everything well. LN*54735, (6)

Envy: If you are envious, projects don't come out how you would like. If you are being envied, people admire you. LN*5547, (3)

Estate: Seeing the estate from afar, desire for tranquility. Estate with animals, gains if the animals are in good state. LN*51217, (7)

Eyes: Represents our inner selves, what we think and what we want to do. It says everything about us. It is the contact with our soul. With good vision, you're clear about what you want. Blurry vision, things aren't so clear if you don't use glasses when you're awake. If you use glasses and you see yourself with them and you see clearly, it's an excellent sign. If you don't see well, you'll need find help from someone. Eyes also represent family. Cross-eyed, you have to put in a lot of effort to make money. Red eyes, conflicts with a family member. Discharge from an eye, illness. LN*5751, (9)

Exam: Shows stress from the dreamer. You have to rest. You devote your mind too much into things. If your exam goes well, you will resolve your inconveniences. If it goes poorly, you'll find yourself in an alley without an exit. LN*5614, (7)

Exile: If you are in your home country and see yourself in exile, drastic changes. LN*56935, (1)

Eyebrows: If they are well done and nice looking, you like to flirt. Shaved or little hair, you are not interested in yourself. LN*57523, (4)

Exchange: It is a warning dream if you are a rich business person. If you're not, it's skill in business, for you will need this exchange to accomplish yourself. LN*56389, (4)

Letter F

Fable: If you're in the fable, you wish for good advice or want to give it to someone. LN*61235, (8)

Face: Remember the expression. If the face is happy, that will be your result. LN*6135, (6)

Factory: Working factory, you will have fortune in your business and financial plans. Abandoned factory, failure. Little activity in the factory, losses. LN*61324, (7)

Fairy Godmother: If you have one, desire to resolve your situation. If you are the fairy godmother, you want to help more than you can. Be careful if you try to give or promise more than you can give. LN*61994, (1)

Fake teeth: For teeth that have a root canal treatment, or crowns, if they fall out and you feel pain, it may be that someone really close to you is going through difficulties. They may be sick and/or pass away. LN*61254, (9)

Falcon: For some, it is envy by friends or animals and how versatile and successful you are in your matters. Rapid success in your endeavors. LN*61332, (6)

Family: Dreaming about your family is really good luck, especially if you have a good relationship with them. If not, the necessity to become closer, possibly the relationship will become better. LN*61491, (21)

Fang: Related to seeing close family members, not your direct family. (See teeth). LN*6157, (1)

Falling: Any fall is a sign of obstacles. Coming out unharmed after a fall, you will regain your confidence. If you get back up quickly, that will be your performance. If you get up slowly, it will take longer. If you can't manage to get up and are very harmed, the problem will make you bow down. Ask for help in any matter so you're not going through it alone. This way it will be easier. It's not impossible, but it will take some time. LN*61333, (7)

Falling into the water: Perhaps the person you married is causing you big problems. LN*61337, (2)

Falling into the agitated sea: Falling off a boat means loss of money, especially if you don't see yourself at shore. Disappointment in love. LN*61333, (7)

Fan: You will receive good news. If it is a hand fan and you are fanning yourself or someone is fanning you, they will surprise you with some news soon. It's not a good sign to lose it. You may lose the love of someone you like. LN*615, (3)

Farming: Tough work. If the soil is fertile, long lasting gains for your work. If the soil is arid and dry, scarceness. Prepare for difficult times. With tenacity, you'll get out of them faster if you take control. LN*61943, (5)

Fatten: Fortune, good times, proximity of money. LN*61221, (3)

Fear: If you face it and find out why you're scared, you'll resolve anything you have yet to resolve; defeat if you don't face it. If you wake up with that fear, you'll have a problem that's hard to face. LN*6519, (21)

Feeding: If you are feeding animals, it's good luck. To eat in excess, the opposite. Feeding children, someone may lie to you. LN*65543, (5)

Feet: Balance and stability, the religious part of you. If they are hurt, someone wants to humiliate you. If they are fractured, loss, whether it's money or a loved one. Barefoot, humbleness. LN*6552, (9)

Fingers: Related to you and your family. Index finger, this is you and what happens to this finger is associated with you. Burning it, purification, start of forgotten projects. Middle finger, family. Thumb, God. Ring finger, career. Pinkie, pleasures. LN*69576, (6)

Fishing: Proximity of money or promotion. If the fish is very big, it's fear. LN*69183, (9)

Five: Symbolizes the human body. The legs, arms and head, if it is used intelligently, is a lucky number. If not used intelligently, stay away from people you don't like. It's a masculine odd number of a good star, especially for those whose destiny number is odd. Transformation, everything depends on the situation we find ourselves in. If we have love problems they will resolve in a while. If you are in financial problems, they will go on for more time. If you burn yourself, you will have big problems.

If you don't get hurt, you will be successful from any problem. If you burn yourself but feel good, renovation. LN*6995, (11), and NS*6945, (6)

Fire: Good fortune. If it is your house, passion. For some it is a warning. When you've had this type of dream and you've experienced a fire or possible fire, take precaution in your home and business.

Fights: Generally when we have a conflict with ourselves with what we want and what we do, it's opposite and different. LN*69783, (6)

Fireflies: Mixture of freedom, peace, and creativity of the dreamer. If that's not you, look for it, because something like this is within you and you need it. LN*69955, (7)

Flamenco: If it is you who's dancing flamenco, you will receive money without much effort. LN*63141, (6)

Flames: If they don't harm you, you'll be okay. If they are calm, you'll come out victorious from the problem. If the flames are raging, the contrary is true. If the flames try to harm you but don't, luck is on your side. LN*63146, (2)

Flying: A fortunate dream. It represents ambition, prosperity, and no limits. If you fly without an aircraft, your ambitions have no limit. If you work for another person, promotion at work. If you're a business person, a project that will have lots of profit. If you fall in flight, your efforts will go with you. If you come out unharmed in the fall, you'll have difficulty getting to your goals, but you'll get there. LN*63793, (1)

Fleas: If they suck on your blood, weakness related to your health. Eat better. LN*63511, (7)

Fly: Problems related to your jealousy. LN*637, (7)

Floating: As long as you continue floating, this is a good sign. If you sink or drown, adversities. Dead animal floating, insecurity. LN*63615, (21)

Flour: It's good if you do something productive with it, like baking bread or pastries. On the contrary, if you are only playing with it, you will have financial issues. LN*63639, (9)

Flood: If you see your house flooding, you may have fights with certain enemies or friends. LN*63664, (7)

Flowers: Great bliss if you receive them. Good sign to see flowers. Red flowers mean you are in love; white flowers, peace and happiness in the family. LN*63656, (8)

Fog: Warns of obstacles. If the sun comes out and the fog goes away, so will our problems. LN*667, (1)

Food: There are many interpretations. The most important thing is how you feel when you sleep or when you wake up. That will be your result. If you eat too much or don't have enough to eat, this is not good. LN*6664, (4)

Forest: If you are alone in the forest, this is good luck in everything. If accompanied, possible deception. If you see beautiful big trees, abundance. If you want to get out of the forest but can't find the exit, obstacles. Getting out, socially you maintain good communication. LN*66953, (11)

Formulae: Restless personality, unconformity. If you work with formulae, your dreams may provide you with what you need to come up with that perfect formula. If you are a student, it's the result of your studies. Finding the answer in the formula, it's satisfactory for your plans. If you don't finish the formula in your dream, you will take longer to finish your projects. LN*66943, (1)

Forehead: Shows honor, intellect, and well being. If it is deformed, it's the contrary. LN*66958, (7)

Four: Number of stability, like a table, that has four legs. Good year, emotional and financial stability. LN*6639, (6)

Fox: A rival will appear in your emotional or business life. If he's dead, you'll win. LN*666, (9)

Fraud: Warning dream if the person who commits fraud is not you,. Be careful with your employees or people you overly trust. If you know who it is in the dream, investigate them to resolve your doubts. If it is you who commits fraud, success. LN*69134, (5)

Friend: Depends on the relationship you have with your friend. If you have been distanced, it's time to call them and resolve your issues. If you are fine, you will run into them soon. Analyze how they are dressed. If they are well-dressed this is good, but if they are not, this means the relationship you have will deteriorate or they might be going through a rough patch. If something happens to your friend in the dream you may want to tell them as it may be a warning. LN*69959, (2)

Frog: If it jumps, success and promotion. LN*6967, (1)

Fruit: If they are nice and healthy, good sign; rotten, the contrary. LN*69392, (11)

- Eating fruits depends if the fruits are in good condition or not. If they are in season, the plan is ready to implement. If they are not in season, the plan needs more time to be achieved. LN*51293, (3)

Frustration: This is completely opposite. If we are frustrated in the dream, this means happiness and refers to taste, success in business. LN*69314, (5)

Fugue/escape: Escaping from something or escaping from where you were trapped, represents how you feel and you want to escape. You are going through a big issue. If you manage to escape and no one catches you, everything will go well. If you're caught, it will be difficult to get out of the issue. LN*63735, (6)

Funeral: The meaning is the contrary. Don't be scared; you will be successful in your projects. If you see yourself wearing black in a funeral, it is good luck. A family member's funeral, you will have long life and health. LN*63554, (5)

Furniture: Changes you've been waiting for are coming and maybe you've also been saving for some time. Hard material furniture, like a table, analyze and listen to other opinions than your own. LN*63952, (7)

Future: Seeing yourself in the future represents messages which may be for you or someone you know. Pay close attention. There are times you will feel you've been somewhere you think you haven't already been, but you've been there in your dreams. It also happens with people. LN*63235, (1)

Letter G

Gallant: (See famous people). LN*61338, (21)

Game: Betting games aren't a good sign, unless you're only observing them. LN*7145, (8)

Garbage: Like the saying goes, one man's trash is another man's treasure. LN*71924, (5)

Garlic: Depends on the person. If you like garlic, it means good fortune. The contrary means unwanted results. LN*71933, (5)

Garden: Excellent signal for business or personal goals, as long as the garden is nicely manicured. A garden represents nature and happiness in your family. If it's dry, money and family problems. LN*71941, (4)

Gas: Related to where you have your vision. Walking with a gas lamp, vision of your objectives. Turned off, you are bothered and can't find an exit to your problems. LN*711, (9)

Gems: Precious stones are common dreams of some women and their wish to possess them. It is not lucky if they don't desire them. It also depends on the color. Aquamarine, prosperity, spirituality; emerald, hard work; ruby, passion, carnal desires. LN*7541, (8)

Genie: Even though you have various wishes and what you wish for is difficult, you maintain your optimism. Continue being optimistic; everything is possible if you believe. A genie who doesn't grant wishes, you've had a long list of disappointments. In consequence, you've lost hope. Imagine the genie always grants your wishes. LN*75595, (4)

Gentlemanly: If you see yourself acting gentlemanly and courteous, you will chase your goals head on. LN*75521, (2)

Gesture: Gesturing with attitude indicates control. Gesturing with your hands, you are calling for attention from someone you love. LN*75128, (5)

Giant: Seeing yourself giant, high self-esteem. Seeing a giant, a rival. Several giants, obstacles; you have a few problems to resolve. If everyone around you is a giant, your self-esteem is really low. If the giant attacks you and you lose, your problems will absorb you. Beating a giant, triumph over your enemies. LN*79152, (6)

Giraffe: You've been a little bit out of reality. Others may see you as elusive. LN*79918, (7)

Glasses: It's a good sign to put glasses on or see yourself with glasses. If you use glasses, this means nothing. Sunglasses are a good sign if you use them in the sun; however, if you use them inside or in the dark these are internal fears. LN*73117, (1)

Glory: Incomplete. You feel like you have a lot to achieve. LN*73697, (5)

Gluttony: Warning of excesses. LN*73322, (8)

Goat: Possible legal rifts. If the goat is okay, you will be too. The color is important, see colors. LN*7612, (7)

Goatling: A trip is coming. Prepare your suitcase if you want to travel. LN*76126, (4)

Going down: Every fall is a sign of obstacles and falling behind in your plans. LN*76952, (2)

Going to sleep: If you are alone, it means embarrassment. On the street, something is bothering you but will pass. With someone of the same gender and you feel uncomfortable, you worry what they will say. If you know them, you will have a better relationship. Of the opposite sex, it's a good sign, especially if you're going through some sort of problem. LN*76952, (11)

Gold: Precious metal that levels your personality. Need of power and ambition. If you have something golden on, luck in your life. LN*7634, (2)

Grains: Fortunate dream in everything. If they are burning, great losses. LN*79196, (5)

Grandparents: If you see yourself as a grandparent, it is a favorable dream. If you see your grandparents and they are alive, it's good luck in business. If they are dead and appear to be reproaching you, you might be doing something that will cause big problems in the future. LN*79157, (11)

Grapes: Signal of prosperity and wealth. White grapes, good sign, especially for sick people; black grapes, destabilization, wrong use of money, and other things. LN*79176, (3)

Letter H

Hail: Big calamities if you come out injured, depending on the damage the hail causes. If you come out unharmed, everything will pass. LN*8193, (21)

Hair: Long hair means abundance; white hair, wisdom, intelligence, this means we are in intellectual projects; dark hair means you are overshadowed and are not looking forward, you are not projecting yourself. Red hair means passion; your thoughts are focused on someone in particular and you can't think about anything else but that person. Shaved head means weakness because of someone or something, embarrassment. LN*8199, (9)

Hallway: Proximity of problems. If the hallway is narrow but you come out of it and have visibility, you'll be fine in every conflict. LN*81334, (1)

Halloween: Give yourself time for the wishes you have withheld for a while. If you see yourself as a child or with many children sharing, your wishes are related to childhood things. LN*81338, (5)

Ham: Gains, as long as it's good. Rotten, losses. LN*814, (4)

Hammock: If you have it in your house, remember why you bought it and how you feel when you lay in it. This will have a lot to do with its meaning. Related to small losses without much importance that you will soon recover and they will be double. LN*81442, (1)

Hanger: You're ready for new obligations like a new job, opening your own business, getting married, or having children. A closet without hangers, fear of taking on responsibilities. LN*81575, (8)

Happiness: Good luck in everything. LN*81773, (8)

Harem: Related to gossip. Don't talk about your personal life to anybody for some time. LN*81954, (9)

Head: You are thinking with your brain and that is good because you are planning what you want and are going to do. Superiority towards others if your head is up. If your head is down, this is humiliation; regretting something you've done is a bad sign. Headache or hitting your head, mental or emotional problems. Bald head, intelligence and love. LN*8514, (9)

Heaven: Seeing yourself in heaven, you are living nice moments and are harmonious in various aspects of your life. If this is not the case, find internal happiness and read self help books. LN*85141, (1)

Heights: If you are scared to look down, it tells you to overcome these fears. If the fear of heights is in others, tackle your problems. If you see yourself fearing heights, you have a fear of falling, because you are not stable either in your love life or work life. Envy, someone wants what you have. LN*85972, (4)

Helping: Many people love you and think well of you. LN*85373, (8)

Hen: Good sign in everything if you see the eggs, and the more eggs the better. Hen with a golden egg, gains, royalties for a short period. LN*855, (9)

Herbs: Everything related to nature is a good sign, especially if the herbs have a nice smell and are beautiful. LN*85921, (6)

Highway: If it is wide, this is good, you have a wider vision of things. If it is narrow, the way you are seeing things is narrow too; you are limiting yourself. The color of the car is important because it represents what you want to know. If you drive off the highway and the car isn't damaged, you have a good team. A straight highway means a long life. LN*89782, (7)

Home: It's good luck seeing your own house, especially if it brings you good memories. If bad memories or empty home, family disgrace. LN*8645, (5)

Horse: Strength and dominion. If you fall, problems await. If you get up unharmed, you'll be fine. If in a horse race, don't look at your business as a game, and be careful not to blow through your money. White horse, overcoming of obstacles, good luck. LN*86915, (11)

House: Seeing it in construction, fortunate dream, realization of a project. The bigger the construction, the bigger your satisfaction. In demolition, losses, have caution in general. Seeing your house empty, abandonment from your kids. They're leaving because they've grown up or because of divorce. Your house filled with things, decorated and clean, progress and happiness. Childhood home, fond memories if you were happy. If you weren't, need to resolve or confront an enigma. LN*86315, (5)

Howls: After the storm comes the calm, calmness after a stormy matter. LN*86531, (5)

Hug: It's not very good luck to be hugged, generally it results in the contrary; however, if you see your partner hug another person, it means good luck. If you give the hug, possible unsatisfied wishes. Hug a dead person for a long life, receive a hug from the dead, illness of the dreamer or possible death. LN*837, (9)

Hunger: It's common to be hungry in a dream if you've just started a diet. If not, this isn't a good sign. LN*83575, (1)

Hunchbacked: If you see a hunchback in your dream, you will have changes in your matters and projects. They will be watching your actions. Ln*83537, (8)

Letter I

Iceberg: If you crash into it or it doesn't let you pass, you will confront giant obstacles and only your distress will get you out of that difficulty. If you pass the iceberg, triumph after putting your strength to the test. LN*93523, (4)

Idols: Take precaution with whom you show your feelings. LN*94631, (5)

Iguana: Coldness, enemies. Depends also on the color. Light is good sign. Dark, love problems. LN*97316, (8)

Image: Unfortunate in one or several aspects, depending on how many images you've seen. Avoid exposing yourself to decisions and conflicts for some time. LN*94176, (9)

Inca: Free spirit for some and for others the desire to find happiness. You'll know which one applies to you by asking yourself two questions: Are you happy? Are you a free and spiritual being? Maybe you want to be at that point of your life and your dreams are moving in the direction of what you need to find your inner you. If you have been reading about the topic, disregard this dream. LN*9521, (8)

Income: If you receive money in your hands generally it points to the contrary. It's important to see how the dream progresses. If it's counting money, not a bad sign. Losing it, you will lend money you will not get back. LN*95369, (5)

Incubator: You will be triumphant in your business, projects, or personal goals in general. LN*95332, (4)

Infidelity: When your loved one is being unfaithful, this means long life to your marriage, as long as it's your subconscious, and it's not actually happening. It also reflects insecurity if you are jealous. LN*95693, (4)

Infinity: Changes relating the future, possible trip. If constellations appear, surprises. Avoid speculation, for surprises can be good or bad. LN*95695, (6)

Immortal: Virile, strong like an oak. You'll be in optimal condition, if you dream that you are the immortal. LN*95466, (3)

Insect: Uncomfortable situation related to work. LN*95155, (7)

Internet: Great skill in communication, great distrust. If you're not distrustful, your dreams are advising you to take this attitude and take action. LN*95253, (7)

Intestine: Animal intestine, common in people who work in places where animals are slaughtered. If your intestines are moldering, fear of stopping because of adversities. If you are experiencing pains in your intestines, this is a warning dream. Go to the doctor. LN*95254, (7)

Island: If you see yourself alone on an island, difficulties that you've created yourself. If you manage to escape, you will resolve the issue. LN*91319, (5)

Letter J

Jade: Gains. If only you see it, your gains will only come with big effort. If you have the jade around your neck, you'll receive money. Selling the jade, possible loss. If it is gifted, you'll receive presents or inheritance. LN*1145, (11)

Jaguar: Distrust in someone that results in confusion. LN*11731, (4)

Jealous: Selfish, your matters are priority without others mattering. LN*15131, (2)

Jesus: One of the most beautiful dreams, predicts positive change for the dreamer. If it's a young person who sees Him, they will change their character and way of seeing life, predicts miracles and big happiness. If you see Him in a specific city, it's improvement of that city. If it's a pregnant woman, she will have a child she will be proud of for life. You will have a long period of prosperity and happiness.

Jewels: Favorable for those in love, couples, or businesspeople, whether you are gifted them or you gift them. If a person tries to rob them from you, someone wants to rob you. LN*15554, (2)

Jockey: Seeing yourself on your horse and winning, everything you put your mind to do will be easy. If you lose, someone is lying to you. LN*16323, (6)

Jumping: You may experience some obstacles. If you see yourself passing those obstacles, you will be successful in your plans. LN*13473, (9)

Jungle: Represents our inner selves, our self-esteem, how sure we are of ourselves. Ask yourself if you were scared. Did the sounds or darkness scare you? If your answer is yes, you need to work more on yourself. If everything was nice and illuminated, you have a good relationship with your inner self. LN*13578, (6)

Letter K

Karaoke: You need to be someone who stands out from the crowd, regardless of what you have to do. If the lyrics are romantic, you desire someone who values you and are willing to do something you're not used to doing. Flowing song, you'll be a better version of yourself, learning new attitudes for your benefit. LN*21914, (8)

Karate: If it's you practicing karate, discipline and assurance. White garb, mental strength. Red, fury, fear of being threatened. The garb is black and not the belt, desire to win no matter what, regardless of who you have to run over. LN*21917, (2)

Kayak: Depends on the conditions of the sea/water and the skill you have while maneuvering the kayak. If the water is murky, difficulties related to what you see. If the water is clear and serene, fortune from what pleasures you. If it is easy for you, everything relating your physical work is in your favor. Hard to manage or you fall in the water, difficulties in resolving a project. LN*21712, (4)

Kilo: Refers to your bodyweight, your image worries you. Kilo of a product you weigh, you think your ideas are not completely fulfilled and you have to add more to them if the weight is too little. If it weighs too much, you or the project are worth a lot. LN*2936, (2)

Kilometer: If you see the distance of where you're headed is short, those will be your goals.If the distance is greater, it will take longer to achieve them. LN*29367, (9)

Kitchen: Preparing food, separation that will end up in divorce. The gas is on, good times and changes in your favor. Grilling, changes in your plans that will disappoint. LN*29239, (7)

Kiss: Depends where you are given the kiss. A kiss on the cheek is friendship but can also be hypocrisy, it all depends on the person giving you the kiss. A kiss on the lips from the person you love is love and good fortune. Sensuality and achieved satisfaction if the kiss is from someone you like and you are a woman. If you are a man, only if it is meant to be, otherwise it will remain in your wishes. On the forehead, friendship, ties, depending on the person who gives it to you. If it is a person with whom you have a bad relationship, you will have a conflict with that person. At the same time, you may want to work on your relationship. LN*2911, (4)

Knees: If they're healthy, showing them is good luck. If they're hurt, financial disaster. LN*25551, (9)

Kneeling: This is good whether it's in your house, in Church, or praying. Something you have been asking for will be fulfilled. LN*25556, (5)

Knife: This has a lot to do with emotions, control yourself. Broken knife means disappointment. Cutting yourself with a knife, you are losing control of your emotions; calm down. LN*25965, (9)

Letter L

Labyrinth: You're confused in your life; don't jump into things too quickly. There's a trap someone wants you to fall into. Think and analyze every step you take. LN*31276, (21)

Lactation: For women, sweetness. If you just had a baby and don't breastfeed, try not to feel guilty about not doing it. For men, desires related to the opposite sex. LN*31325, (5)

Lake: Everything that has to do with water. If the water is clear and calm, you will enjoy peace and tranquility in your home. If it's murky, there are problems. LN*3125, (11)

Lamp: Need to be with happy people, even though you have a certain distrust. Without a bulb, broken, or it doesn't work, you've lost all interest in everything. LN*3147, (5)

Language: If two or more people are speaking a different language than yours, you are introverted and should communicate more. If you speak a different language than others, lack of communication. Someone teaching you a new language, possible trip abroad. LN*31577, (5)

Lark: To listen to it means achieved pleasures. To see it in a cage means possible failure in financial matters you have caused yourself. I recommend you revise your plan to improve your charitable side. This will change the course of your business even if this dream is just a warning. LN*3192, (6)

Lawyer: If you see a lawyer you might have difficulties. If you are the lawyer, you will cause difficulties for another person. LN*31575, (21)

Learning. It's good for business to see yourself learning something new. If it is too difficult for you, you've bit off more than you can chew. It will be hard to finish if you don't take necessary measures. LN*35198, (6)

Letter: If you receive a letter, this is bad news. If you send it, you want yourself to be known somehow. Receiving a letter from a loved one or someone you like, commitment, perhaps an upcoming relationship. If it's from a person you have a good relationship with it's good news. LN*35225, (8)

Lice: If they're on your head and they sting, numerous small problems. If you kill them, you'll be successful in work matters, proximity of money. Other people, you have sympathy for others and their problems. LN*3935, (2)

Light up: Excellent dream if you're involved in a project or want to achieve one. If you see yourself with pain or the project goes slowly, keep going because in the end you will persevere. LN*39783, (3)

Lightning Bolt: Unexpected reward. LN*39781, (1)

Lips: Beautiful and healthy lips reflect health in the dreamer and those who surround them. The contrary implies illness. If you are a man and you dream about a woman's sensual lips, you have a need for love from the opposite sex. You've been with few people or have had too many flings. LN*3971, (2)

Lipstick: Desire to attract the opposite sex. For some, it means desire to improve their image. LN*39717, (9)

Lion: To be the lion, wisdom, power. If you're attacked or chased by the lion, problems with someone you see superior to you. Battling with the lion and winning, triumph over something almost impossible to win. LN*3965, (5)

Living room: You'll have changes soon and you'll have to make one or more decisions if the room is big. If it's empty, abandonment, you feel this way. LN*39491, (4)

Lizard: Animals that crawl, whether they are reptiles, snakes, or lizards, show the negative side of other people or the dreamer. Be careful, for you have an enemy. If you use its skin, you'll have success over your enemies and good fortune. LN*39814, (7)

Losing your job: It's very common to have this type of dream because of work stress, the news, and other stressors. Generally, it doesn't mean you'll lose your job, but you worry about it. If you haven't thought about the matter, it means you might not be doing your job properly. LN*36191, (2)

Loan: For some it's good, as is a loan to buy a house. It reflects organization, growth. Loan to cover your expenses, you feel drowned. You've lost faith in yourself and your possibilities. LN*3615, (6)

Losing weight: Problems, perhaps health issues or financial may be coming, whether it is the dreamer who loses weight or animals, which represents poverty and scarcity. But if you see yourself fat or see fat animals, it's a sign of wealth and abundance. Obese, a sign to change your diet. It means you must lose weight if you are obese or you may be suffering from anorexia if you are underweight. LN*36193, (4)

Lottery: Desire to win it, you have something within yourself to discover. Take advantage of this and wish for more. Write down the winning numbers and buy them. It's possible you'll fall in love and find commitment. LN*36223, (7)

Love: For some it is the contrary if you are in a relationship, but good for those who are not. Misery in love is rather good. If it is love amongst friends, this means bliss. LN*3645, (9)

Lover: If you are a woman, it means achievement of a future relationship, if you don't have anything serious at the moment. If you are a man, this depends on the dream. It may be only a wish and you are scared of rejection. LN*36459, (9)

Loving (adj): Possible treason, gossip if it is you who is very loving. LN*36493, (7)

Loyal: It's contradictory to infidelity, treason. Don't trust too much. LN*36713, (2)

Letter M

Magnet: You are in all your splendor, relating to the law of attraction. Do positive repetitions of what you wish for and what you wish to attract, for you can attract something in your life you don't want when you simply think about something or fearing something. Use it in your favor, not against you. LN*41757, (6)

Manicure: If you're getting a manicure, possible commitment with someone much older than you. If you're giving the manicure, desire to get married. LN*41592, (21)

Manuscripts: Not very good signs. You have to see what is written and if you like it or not, because it may be a discovery. LN*41535, (9)

Mare: The same meaning as the horse. Usually depends on the color of the horse or mare. White, favorable news. Grey, obstacles. LN*4195, (1)

Mars: Iron, like the planet. Your life is fine, but you haven't made many good friends. You feel as if you want to go to another planet. Strong and explosive temper. LN*4191, (6)

Metals: Each one must be identified separately. Copper is oppression. Bronze, not good fortune. Gold, you'll be successful and powerful. You have to be careful, it's a warning in money, worries. LN*45214, (7)

Millionaire: Depends on your current situation. If you are okay, proximity of money, you are positive and believe in yourself. If you're not okay, frustrations. Analyze yourself, for you will have to make money work for you, and not you working for the money. LN*49338, (9)

Mirror: Treason on our part or treason from other people toward us, depending on who is looking into the mirror. LN*49996, (1)

Mice: Difficulties with friends or partners. A cat that kills a mouse, you'll come out victorious over who causes or wishes you ill. If they are trapped, people talk badly about you. If it's a dog and it catches a mouse, your problems will be over. LN*4935, (3)

Mock-up: Your mind is creative and restless. Take advantage of this time in your life. You'll earn a lot of money if you take advantage of your creativity. LN*46321, (7)

Money: Seeing money is always a good sign and finding it is even better. Satisfactions will be met not only related to money, but also to family matters. If you are robbed, it's a bad sign. If you are counting money and are missing some, you are short on your payments. In people with financial needs, this reflects ungranted wishes and desires. Counting big banknotes and handing them out to family members, financial betterness, fortune for you and for your family. You are very generous. LN*46557, (9)

Monkey: Proximity of problems for some. For others, the reflection of being prepared in life for alternatives. If you have a problem, resolve it one way or another. It's a warning. LN*46523, (2)

Monsters: Nightmares and proximity of conflicts, illnesses. If we are sore, ate too much, bad digestion, or mental problems. Consequences of what we've seen or heard. LN*46518, (1)

Moon: Feminine intuition, renovation, a hidden side to discover, physical and emotional power of the dreamer. If the moon is beautiful and shining and the sky is clear, happiness in love and bliss. Full moon, cloudy and opaque, the contrary. Full moon and clear skies is good for love, as is a new moon for business. LN*4665, (21)

Mountain: A positive sign, shows wealth and achievement of our goals. LN*46358, (8)

Mouth: The way we express ourselves. If the mouth is closed, whether it's ours or someone else's, this represents the rejection of someone towards us or our own towards another person. Mouth open, this is a positive sign towards creativity and thirst to express ourselves in some aspect. LN*46328, (5)

Mother: Common dream. Mother happy with you, she is happy in what you've become. Not happy, bad communication. Death, isn't bad, but maybe there's a distance between you physically, not emotionally. LN*46285, (7)

Mud: If you see yourself working with the mud, you will create something with big benefits. If you see someone else, this also means financial benefits, but not necessarily of your own creation. LN*434, (11)

Mushrooms: In the forest, everything related to nature attracts you or you are in need of going away to relax. Seeing them, you will adapt quickly to a situation. Eating them, desire to experience new things. LN*43188, (6)

Myopia: Lack of focus in your plans and in your future. Buying glasses, you're aware of your disadvantages and are looking for a plan B. LN*47671, (7)

Letter N

Nausea: Warning you may have problems. NS*51316, (7)

Nails: Success, whether it's finger or toe nails. If you cut them wrong, you'll have problems and you'll be destabilized. If it's toenails, if you cut them normally and not too short you'll be okay. LN*51931, (1)

Needles: Small discomforts, whether it be love, gossip, with an exception if the needle has a thread through it. If you poke yourself, you're too in love and show it too much. Tone it down a bit. LN*55549, (1)

Nest: Excellent for business if there are eggs or newborns. Empty, a long way to go for your project. Someone destroys it or eats the babies, big losses. LN*5512, (4)

Neurons: Need to receive stimulation. Related at times to the nervous system. Uncontrol in your life. Relax with any kind of exercise like yoga or going out to get fresh air. LN*55393, (7)

Night: As always, darkness is a bad sign. LN*59782, (4)

Nightmares: A consequence of different factors (see chapter on nightmares). LN*59784, (6)

Nose: In good state, everything's going fine. Nosebleed, financial problems. If you see yourself in your home, family conflicts. LN*5615, (8)

Notary: You'll have over your shoulders the responsibility of others if you are the notary. If someone else is the notary, you'll have problems understanding documents. Read what you are given thoroughly and don't sign anything until you are certain what you're signing. LN*56217, (3)

Nudity: The less clothes you have on the better, better financial status, sensuality, and desires. Not being embarrassed of anything in life, accepting oneself. LN*53499, (3)

Numbers: Practical and calculating person, the creation and start of everything. Everything needs a number. If you see symbols of the same figure, add them and the people you see. Record each number individually, not in even or odds, and don't go past number nine. LN*53426, (2)

- One: Symbolizes creation. The first number, like the start of anything we're going to do, number of force.

- Number one: (see number) Number of all beginning, selfishness. Masculine number, individuality.

- Number two: Feminine number, even number that represents couples, number of balance and stability. LN*256, (4)

- Two: Twin souls, things similar to everything in pairs or couples.

- Three: They say three is the perfect number, but it can also mean a conflict that can be solved by a third person, like a referee. It can also represent the opposite. Infidelity, a third person is the negative part. LN*28955, (11)

- Four: It's the most stable. Like a table with four legs, it's harder to fall down. Represents stability. LN*6639, (6)

- Five: Symbolizes the human body. The legs, arms, and head, if it is used intelligently is a lucky number. On the contrary, stay away from people you don't like. It's a masculine odd number of a good star, especially for those whose destiny number is odd. LN*6945, (6)

- Six: Spiritual number, symmetry, the sixth part of the body, the sixth sense. LN*196, (7)

- Eight: Stable, infinity. LN*59782, (4)

- Nine: Culmination of the project we are involved in. LN*5955, (6)

Nurse: You worry about someone close to you getting ill. Their clothing is important. See colors for better interpretation. LN*53915, (5)

Nuts: Wish that will soon be granted. Nuts on a tree, family happiness. LN*5321, (11)

Letter O

Oasis: You have loyal friends. LN*61191, (9)

Oats: In the field and in harvest, this means abundance. If they are stale and dry, difficult times are coming, and you should save money. LN*6121, (1)

Obstacle: Warning dream of difficulties. If you beat the obstacles, this will mean the contrary. Look for help to overcome them. LN*62124, (6)

Oculist: They're watching you if you visit the oculist, just like the need for someone to help you resolve your issues. LN*63333, (9)

Office: If you have problems or worries, related to work or love. Post office, positive changes. Unexpected, possible change of residence. LN*66698, (8)

Oil: Success and fortune for women or people who use it frequently, like painters, cooks, etc. On the contrary, it is unfortunate, but if you take it, or if it is poured on your head, improvement in your matters related to mental work. LN*693, (9)

Old person: To see the elderly is one of the wisest dreams there is. It reflects maturity in the dreamer. Culmination of a project. LN*63477, (9)

Operation: There is a problem you must tackle and it relates to what is being operated on in the dream. Heart, love problems. You must end that relationship. Obviously, you should verify you don't have any health issues, because this dream can also be a health warning. LN*67595, (5)

Opening: Sign of hope. LN*67553, (8)

Opponent: You'll encounter certain conflicts, if you have a rival. If not, they're related to family or problems with your partner. If you have a rival, you have to confront them, and ask them questions to decipher mysteries. LN*67768, (7)

Orange: Orange tree, related to sincere and beautiful love, if the tree has fruit and in good condition. The contrary means the opposite. LN*69153, (6)

Orchestra: It's good luck to hear sounds of instruments that are part of an orchestra. If you are not spiritual, it is the desire to be spiritual. LN*69389, (8)

Ostrich: Take on your responsibilities and don't hide now that the sun can't be covered with a single finger. LN*61292, (2)

Overflowing river: Seeing your house flood, possible arguments with friends or enemies. LN*64599, (5)

- Water is rising and the river overflows, good news, depending on what one does. For example, if you have a legal issue, it will be resolved, if it is divorce, or any other problem. Related to work or other legal matters.

Owl: Good vision in business. LN*653, (5)

Ox: Good sign regarding speculation. You will be lucky, but always consult a specialist. If the ox is sick, don't buy or sell your stocks or business for some time. LN*66, (12)

Letter P

Pacifier: Good family luck and a possible new member of the family. LN*71392, (4)

Pain: Reflects regret of the dreamer; something the dreamer may have done consciously or unconsciously. If the pain is small, it is related to health. If the pain is deep, possible financial gains as long as the dreamer has not done anything to anyone recently. LN*7195, (5)

Parents: Reflects that you must solve past problems or connect more with them, if they are a distance from you, not necessarily because you don't speak, but because of the actual distance. LN*71958, (3)

Partner: If you see your partner kiss someone else, as long as you don't know them, don't worry. If the dream is recurring regarding your partner, analyze your behavior. LN*71921, (2)

Past: It's common to dream about your childhood home, and the interpretation depends on how your childhood was, and if it's related to your emotions. Shows melancholy, memories, wishes. It may relate to conflicts you must heal if you went through something upsetting. Go back in time and heal that wound and forgive the person who hurt you. LN*7112, (11)

Path: If it is a wide path with lots of visibility, those are the opportunities that are coming your way. A narrow path with low visibility means few alternatives. One that is destroyed means conflict. LN*7128, (9)

People you know: Seeing people you know and you have good relations with them, good luck. If you see your enemies, you might be exposed to public mockery. Family members, happiness. LN*75676, (4)

Persecution (see nightmares): Close to conflict, you're running away from reality or something else. LN*75916, (1)

Photographs: Negative for some and positive for others; could indicate treason. Beautiful photos, treason. Blurry, uncertain future. Seeing your own photo and liking it is good. Partner taking photos, they are lying to you. LN*78623, (8)

Pig: Controversial, things can go well or badly for you. If the pig is fat, it means gains. If scrawny, debt. Different pigs, various projects; some will work out, some won't. LN*797, (5)

Pirana: Restlessness, internal problems. A lot of them biting you, regrets that take away your peace. LN*79916, (5)

Plane: Plane accident, related to a project that hasn't yet been completed and will be incomplete or will go down, depending on what happens in the dream. Depends on how you are feeling in your life. If you see the plane or you are inside, money is coming and so are big projects. Being the pilot means you have self control, symbolizes intellect and elevated ideas that you need to be free to think. LN*73155, (21)

Police: If they come to help you, it's good luck. Someone will help you out of an issue or conflict. If you're the aggressor and they come to arrest you, beware of bad conduct. LN*76397, (5)

Poplar: You will receive financial gains. LN*76731, (6)

Port: For those who are successful, that feeling of accomplishment represents an end to a phase and the start of a new goal that will be very productive. If you aren't accomplished, this represents your melancholic past with a promising future. LN*7692, (6)

Prank: Desire to expand your friendships. LN*79152, (6)

Pregnancy: Good dream, especially if you are in the middle of a project, idea, or starting one, for it will soon come to light. Complications in the pregnancy, you will have obstacles before finishing your project. LN*79573, (4)

Purple: Color of royalty, wealth, and love. LN*73978, (9)

Purse: Empty, you will soon receive money. Filled and you see yourself checking the inside, you will know about a secret. Carrying it means news. Old, broken, and dirty means problems. LN*73915, (7)

Putting out a fire with water, throwing water: This may be a defeat in a trial. It could go well or badly, depends on how you are handling the situation. LN*73223, (8)

Letter Q

Letter R

Railway: Changes in your favor, whether they're for you alone or with family members or someone else. LN*91934, (8)

Rain: If it rains a lot, love problems. It's best to avoid arguments with your partner. Good sign if the rain isn't strong. If it's clear and the sky is too, wealth, well being for those who work in the field, good times for their harvest. If it's heavy rain, the sky is dark. This is bad luck; you'll have a problem in your work. LN*9195, (6)

Rainbow: An excellent dream. You have or will have good fortune in love, matrimony, or family. LN*91954, (1)

Rage: Bad mood. If you lose your marbles without reason, you're stressed and need to take a break and think about what you're doing. LN*9175, (4)

Rake: Hard working person, you like to be in contact with nature and tranquility. Plant something; it will help you more than you think. If this is your profession, this dream is very common for you. LN*9125, (8)

Rape: Warning dream only for young girls who are still virgins. Beware of men with bad intentions, someone with bad intentions surrounds you, someone who doesn't deserve your love, disappointment. If the dreamer is not young, whether male or female, prosperity. LN*9175, (4)

Rat: If it's white, everything will go okay and you'll have success in your projects. If it's brown, you'll possibly encounter difficulties and an enemy. If it's more than one rat, the problem is bigger than what you imagine and possibly out of your hands. If you're in a couple, a rival is coming. LN*912, (12)

- Dead rat: If the problem resolves, it's not that big. Negative: A new problem is born. Depends on the dreamer, what they do, and what position they are in life. If you are a businessperson, a big project is coming and you have to put in the effort. If you do it, something bigger than what you imagine will be born. Housewife, problems that will be resolved for your husband or kids. LN*45143, (8)

Record player: You're restless or a very active person. Need to be closer to family. LN*95369, (5)

Red meat: Eating red meat is related to speculation and investments. The more well done the meat is, without being burnt, the better. If it is raw, don't jump into speculations and investments. If you thoroughly vet them, you'll have good gains. LN*95448, (3)

Recurring dream (See recurring dreams): LN*95337, (9)

Rice: Like all grains, it means happiness. LN*9935, (8)

Ring: For a young unmarried girl, engagement. A married woman dreaming of a ring means conflict

Your Dreams and You

with her husband. If she takes it off, tosses it, or loses it, they will separate. If she finds it, they'll have a serious argument, but will reunite. LN*9957, (3)

River: Rivers are like different times of our lives, like currents in the path they flow in. If you swim against the current and can't get to where you want, you can't go against the problem. The best option is to tackle the problem even if you don't like it. If you go with the current, that demonstrates favor in your life. LN*99459, (8)

Rollercoaster: It's an example of our lives. If you see yourself going up, you're fine. Be prepared for the fall that plummets faster than going up. LN*96359, (5)

Robbery: Warning dream. Check your house and business for possible robbery. Someone wants what you have. If you're the one who robs, don't wish for what isn't yours. Envy. LN*96223, (4)

Rooster: It's good to listen to a rooster in the morning, for your plans will happen when you've planned them. If it sings at night, something isn't right. LN*96617, (11)

Rubber bands: Flexibility and an active life. In a bad state, delays in your plans. Several, the result is duplicated. LN*93229, (6)

Running: If you are running alone and you reach your destination or goal, good fortune awaits you. If you are running away from something and you don't know what, these are problems for which you don't know the source. Think wisely about what you're going to do. Running naked without a reason is a psychological problem, dementia. LN*93553, (7)

Ruins: It's the contrary; money and security are coming. LN*93951, (9)

Letter S

Letter S: Letter of power, transmutation, changes in your favor. Renovation of your life or a family member's. If the letter appears in the sky, divine power; you'll receive a miracle. LN* (1)

Salt: Good times. LN*1132, (7)

Samurai: If you're the Samurai, you sacrifice yourself for your loved ones and they see in you a person of positive values. Seeing one, desire to have nobleness and have people loyal to you. LN*11431, (1)

Sand: If you see sand in the sea, this is good. If not, these are various annoyances. Mixing sand will depend on what you are mixing it with; if it is with cement, you will concrete your dreams. If it becomes watery, this is the contrary, and points to more annoyances. LN*1154, (2)

- Quick sand: Be more aware of your actions or they will bury you. LN*83934, (9)

Sandal: You feel free. If you don't feel this way, you desire it; liberate yourself. LN*11544, (6)

Sanatorium: Avoid being in a business where they try to manipulate you. Make your own decisions without being obligated. LN*11517, (6)

Santa Claus: Fantasy and desire in children who believe in Santa Claus. LN*11538, (9)

Sapphire: Power, integrity, healing of any evil. LN*11774, (2)

Saving: Fear of losing money. Recommend you ignore this dream. LN*11493, (9)

Sea: The sea is like your conscious and subconscious, your fertile part. If it's strong, you are in conflict, having certain problems that you must resolve. If the waves are too big, your problems are even bigger. LN*151, (7)

Seawater: To have it with you, affection. To lose it, disappointment. To buy it, happiness. LN*15158, (11)

Seagull: Flying, desire, or achievement of freedom. Fishing, focus, power over your adversities. Still, stress, you need to rest or you may get ill. LN*15176, (2)

Secret: Keeping them and not spilling them represents trust, associated at the same time with being a bit introverted. Spilling them, people and your friends don't trust you anymore. LN*15397, (7)

Selling: If you sell at a high price, success in business. Selling below the price, you'll have financial struggles. Be careful with your expenses. LN*15393, (21)

Sending: Usually when you give, you receive; you are waiting for good news. Determine that what you wish for you will receive, so you can attract only what you want. LN*15543, (9)

Shark: You'll resolve and come out okay from a problem. If it bites or scratches you, certain conflicts are coming, but you'll go forward. LN*18192, (3)

Snake: Gossip, problems that are coming in your house or work. Beware of gossip; don't talk badly about anyone. It'll multiply against you. LN*15125, (5)

- Snake with several heads: The same as the snake but in complicity. Take more care of yourself; someone is plotting something; try to kill it in your dream. LN*15123, (12)

Separation: If your marriage isn't well, it's a product of your subconscious, or you've heard about the topic regarding another person too. If all is well in your marriage, it may be your conscience reminding you of something you've done, and you still feel guilty. LN*15715, (1)

Sex: Common dream. If we have sex with someone of the same sex, it refers to something that person has that we admire. If it's with your family, don't take it the wrong way; you'll get closer to that family member. If it's a woman and the person who you're with, you like it and it's a possible granting of your wishes. If it's a man, immediate granting of wishes. LN*156, (3)

Sexual organ: Healthy, a good sign. Deformed, family problem. If it's a woman's, it refers to successful children. A man's, embarrassment, problems in the ovaries, they hurt. It points to your own illness or your son's. It's possible someone wants to harm you. LN*15635, (2)

Scale/balance: You are a person who tries to be fair. You may be called upon to testify for someone. LN*13135, (4)

Scaring people: If you are the person who does the scaring, you like to surprise others. Be careful who you surprise; analyze the attitude of whom you've surprised and that will be your result. If you've been scared and you liked it, you like being surprised. If you didn't like it, something negative is coming or will be discussed in your life. LN*13193, (8)

School: Being in school shows stress in the dreamer or childhood memories. If you are in school, you have worries. If you are in business, new projects. LN*13869, (9)

Shaving: Possible financial losses. If you are shaving your head, something is troubling you. LN*18143, (8)

Sheet: Depends on the color of the sheet. If it's a gift to you, it's good. Dirty, money loss. LN*18552, (21)

Sheep: You've planned, and now you'll pick up your fruits thanks to your planning and organization. Selling them, losses. LN*18557, (8)

Ship full of people: Changes in your work or opinion on something or someone. Analyze if you have good relations or not, how people are dressed, and the color of their garments. Observe if the water is crystal clear; in this case, the change will be good. Otherwise, the change may be negative. LN*18971, (8)

Shipwreck: Disappointment in love, uncontrollable passions, or possible conflicts. LN*18976, (4)

Shoes: New shoes, new projects with good alternatives, clean, success. Dirty shoes, illnesses, conflicts. Broken shoes, financial imbalance, poverty. Barefoot, submission or success. LN*18651, (21)

Shot gun: If it is in a perfect state, everything will go well. If it is in disrepair, that's how your plans will go. LN*18626, (5)

Sibling: If you have a good relationship with them and are on good terms in the dream, it is long lasting happiness. If you fight, you will have certain family arguments. LN*19233, (9)

Sinking: Shows the status of your goals. If you try to come up to the surface and you reach it, you will resolve your problems. If not, you will have great conflicts. LN*19523, (2)

Skill: Developing a skill you don't possess, they will soon honor you for an achievement you hadn't been honored for before. It can also be an insufficiency you have, and you have to learn something new that you like, and you haven't had the money to do it until now. LN*12933, (9)

Skinny: If you see yourself skinny and you like it, you are happy with your physical appearance. This is good, for this is good for your self-esteem. If you are too skinny, you will have financial losses. Try not to spend money on unnecessary things. LN*12953, (11)

Sky: Clear and sunny skies represent aspirations, authority, prosperity, and plenty. Dark skies mean conflicts are going away. Going to heaven means a big wish will be granted. LN*127, (1)

Slap: If we slap, we will have negative consequences, because we may be wrong in one of our actions. If we are slapped, maybe someone is being unfair towards us. LN*1317, (12)

Sleeping: If we see ourselves sleeping, it reflects that we are distracted. We have to pay a bit more attention. Sleeping with someone of the opposite sex means everything is going okay. Husband and wife sleeping together with a third person in their bed means marriage problems. LN*13551, (6)

Slim down: Take care of your health and your finances. You may have neglected one of the two. LN*13941, (9)

Smells: Nice smell, peace and harmony. Bad smell, fear of not being accepted. Bad breath, be careful with what you say. You may talk too much. Verify if you've said something embarrassing. If you actually smell, disregard this dream. LN*14531, (5)

Snow: Because of its whiteness and purity, it is associated to honor, concord, and security. Snow in your house or business, abundance. LN*1565, (8)

Spear: Protect yourself from your enemies. Having the spear in your hands in an attack, you're being competitive. This is good if you use it positively. Not being able to lift it, you have low self-esteem.

Appreciate every single one of your successes. LN*17519, (5)

Spending: This kind of dream is a warning, unless it's December. This is your subconscious telling you what you're doing. Listen to it and don't go too fast. LN*17557, (7)

Sniper: Global vision, focus. Most of the time you like to work on your own and in some occasions keep a low profile. If you see yourself as a sniper without the rifle, you've been preparing yourself for something for a while but are still not ready. Something will go wrong. (Warning dream.) Continue to revise your plan until you find the problem. If you don't, come up with a plan B. LN*15975, (9)

Soap: You will resolve an enigma and clean your exterior if you bathe with it. If you wash your hands, you're like Pontius Pilate. LN*1617, (6)

Sorceress: If it's you, you will be lucky. If you see one and she makes a potion, your friends speak badly about you. LN*16933, (4)

Sour taste: Hardships and disappointments. LN*16392, (3)

Spectacle: This is a positive dream if you don't abandon the spectacle before analyzing if you feel good about it or not. LN*17535, (21)

Spine: If it is healthy, you are in control of your nerves. Curved, warning of illness. LN*17955, (9)

Spouse: (See husband/wife). LN*17636, (5)

Stairs: If you are going up, this is how your life will go. If you are going up too fast, you will reach your goals faster than you anticipated. If you are going up slowly, your goals and wishes will be met, only slowly. If you are going down, your aspirations are also. If it's an unsteady staircase, be sure about your decisions before every step you take. If it's a sturdy staircase, go on with confidence. LN*12191, (5)

Starch: Don't put all your trust in anyone just because they seem trustworthy. Not everything that shines is gold. Look at the inner core of the person you trust, not the outer. LN*12192, (6)

Storage: Generally good fortune, unless the storage is in bad state. LN*12694, (4)

Strangers: As long as there are good interactions with strangers, there is no problem. If you have bad interactions, you will resolve any problem that comes your way. LN*12919, (4)

Steel: Shows security, strength, success. LN*12553, (7)

Stool: You'll receive support from something or someone on a lower scale. LN*12663, (9)

Storm: Emotional changes that will be solved with effort. LN*12694, (4)

Sugar: Nice events, especially with your family. LN*13719, (21)

Sun: It's masculine, superior. If the sun is seen through the clouds and you have a feeling of peace and calm, your problems will be resolved. Sun is success in whatever matter, whether it's work or emotional. If you're pregnant or close to being pregnant, you'll have a boy. LN*135, (9)

Super hero: Superman, power, achievement, vision. Spiderman, power associated to big responsibilities, time to grow. LN*13751, (8)

Super powers: You have high self-esteem. If this isn't the case, they are warning you that you're close to achieving better self-esteem and to continue to work on it. Immortal, power, desire to have a long life. Eat healthy and exercise. LN*13756, (4)

Swimming: If you see yourself swimming with assurance and get to your destination, imminent success awaits you. If you don't reach your destination and you feel like you're drowning and you're scared and swim with difficulty, hard work without much profit awaits you. If you get to the destination swimming with difficulty, even if you go slowly, you'll get to your goal. LN*15947, (8)

Syringe: You feel the need to ask for help in job related matters. LN*17998, (7)

Letter T

Talking: If you know what you are talking about and it has meaning, power of speech. If you don't understand what you're saying or have fear in expressing freely, beware of slander. LN*21323, (2)

Tears: Good sign, for crying cleans us and helps us bring out what we have inside, consolation from others. LN*25191, (9)

Teeth: Front teeth are associated with close family. It means someone in your family may be sick or may die, if these teeth fall out. If it hurts when the tooth falls out, you will be saddened by the death of this family member. If it doesn't hurt, it is a family member with whom you don't have much contact. It also reflects the internal health of the dreamer or someone close. LN*25528, (4)

Thankfulness: Socially you will maintain good relations and comfortable communication. LN*28158, (6)

Thief: Warns of distrust towards others, a warning to revise everything at home or business. If you catch the thief, you'll be successful. If you see them and don't catch them and it's night time or dark, you'll have problems. LN*28956, (3)

Thinning: (See Skinny). LN*28958, (5)

Tiles: Everything you do from now on, make sure you put your name on it so your work can be appreciated, to avoid having someone steal your ideas. LN*29351, (2)

Thread: Working or doing something with thread, fortune thanks to your financial planning in the past. Continue to be organized. Cutting the thread, financial losses due to unexpected events or bad decisions. Untangling thread, you will resolve an event. If another person untangles the knot, you will see how someone who was in a bad place gets on track. LN*28955, (11)

Thorn: If you hurt yourself with a thorn, obstacles. If you're not hurt, you'll be okay. Depends on the part of the body hurt by the thorn. Foot or left hand, your artistic side will have obstacles. If it penetrated deeply, the problem will be harder to solve. If it's superficial, it will be something temporary. The right hand is associated with your analytic side, finances, and work. LN*28694, (2)

Tiger: Refers to obstacles. If it chases and attacks you, loss of money. Listening to the growl of a tiger and you're scared, fear of failure. LN*29759, (5)

Tobacco: Very soon all your problems will vanish. LN*26213, (5)

Toasting (cheering): Fake friends. LN*26115, (6)

Torch: If it is lit up. it means light, focus, revelation about an enigma. If it is unlit, you must take action. LN*26938, (1)

Tornado: Conflicts around you. Depending on the dream, you'll resolve them or not. If the tornado destroys a town, loss of certain employees or friends.

If the tornado comes toward you and suddenly vanishes, you'll resolve your issues with intelligence. LN*26952, (6)

Tooth loss: It affects people in different ways, depending on the circumstances. 1. Front teeth are your close family and the back teeth are cousins, grandparents, and a second family. 2. If it hurts, you'll lose someone in your family. If it doesn't hurt, it's an estranged relative or relative outside your close family. Also related to your personal health or that of a family member. LN*26628, (6)

Toad: Depends on what the toad represents. Whether it's good or disgusting, that will be your interpretation. Jumping, promotion. Poisonous toad, conflicts. Kissing it, need to look for fairy tale love. LN*2614, (4)

Tongs: Problems with people around you. LN*26571, (21)

Torture: You're frustrated because something doesn't let you concentrate and you treat yourself badly. If someone you know is torturing you, it's important to know what this person represents in your life. If it's your partner, you're in a toxic relationship. Could point to children, family problems. LN*26928, (8)

Train: Changes in your life. If the journey is pleasant, your path will be positive. If it's a short trip, you'll be far away from your family. Traveling with your family is family reunification. LN*29195, (8)

Traveling to the moon: Great ambitions. To space, desire to get out of what stresses you. To deserted places, you enjoy your loneliness. If you don't enjoy being alone, it reveals that you need to take some off time to reorganize your life and work on projects you haven't been able to because of lack of time. LN*291452, (5)

Treasure: Loss of money at the same time, multiplied gains. You'll have to use your head to find it. LN*29511395, (8)

Tree: Sign of nature. It's important to pay attention to the condition of the tree. Green and luscious, improvement. Dry or neglected, difficult moments await you. Falling from a tree, your problems are accumulating; find an exit. Climbing a tree and getting to the top, your problems will resolve. LN*2955, (21)

- Tree full of fruit: Currently everything is going well. If you are going through difficulties, they will be resolved.

Trip: Changes in your life, depending on how the dream goes and how you feel when you wake up. If it was good, you'll have a positive change. If you're poor, you'll be rich. If you're single, you'll find the love you've been looking for. If the trip wasn't good, negative changes. Beware of speculations and drastic changes, and watch your temper. Traveling with children, happiness. LN*2997, (9)

Tsunami: Warns of problems related to a bigger weight than you're used to lifting. Be calm and try to manage your stress. LN*2135149, (7)

Tunnel: If it's narrow and dark and you don't come out of it, it will be difficult to solve your issues. If there's light in the tunnel and it's wide and you come out of it, you'll come out okay from a legal matter. LN*235553, (5)

Turtle: Fragile personality with strong appearance on the outside, for some if your temper is explosive. For some, you take too long in making important decisions, but if that isn't your personality, your dream is warning you to adopt said behavior. LN*239235, (5)

Tying: If you are tied up, there is co-dependence on your part. If you untie yourself, this is good, because you will get out of that co-dependance. If it is you who has tied up someone, you are being unfair. If it is someone you like, this means attraction. LN*27957, (12)

Twins: If you dream about them when they are babies, you will have two difficulties. If they are older, success and happiness. LN*25951, (4)

Letter U

Udder: Full of milk, wealth, growth. Empty, it'll take more work or investment to see a profit. LN*34459, (7)

Ugly: Seeing someone ugly is not a bad sign, but if they are deformed, it is. If it bothered you, it is good luck. LN*3737, (2)

Ulcer: Emotional problems. LN*33359, (5)

Uniform: If it's a military uniform, dignity and pride for your country. Uniforms usually mean promotion. LN*3596694, (6)

University: You've come a long way in your life, studies, and aspirations. LN*35945919, (9)

Universe: Success, if fire. If meteorites fall from the universe, catastrophe. The way you sound and feel when you wake up is important for the interpretation. If you feel good and it's positive, unlimited wealth. LN*35945915, (12)

Letter V

Valley: If you go into the valley and don't come out, problems. If you do come out, resolution. At the same time, it's the need to find yourself with nature, as long as it's day time. LN*413357, (5)

Virgin: Different meanings, depending on the circumstances. Virgin giving you her back, you're doing something wrong that your family doesn't agree with. Virgin like an image or facing you, fortunate dream.

Vulture: If it chases you and you are scared, dangerous enemy. Dead, elimination of a rival. If it is devouring its prey, luck is on your side. LN*4332395, (2)

Letter W

Waffle: Satisfaction, especially if you see children eating waffles with honey. LN*516635, (8)

Walking: If you're walking in the daylight, this is a good sign. If you are arriving where want at night, some differences. Walking over water, definite success. LN*5132957, (5)

War: Domestic problems, internal conflicts, and in work. It refers as well to the subconscious if you saw a movie or are going through something similar or a family member is. LN*519, (6)

Washington: Power, ambition if you find yourself in big cities as long as they're in good shape and not destroyed. If you go around the city, your ambitions will be achieved. LN*51189574, (4)

Watch: If it's a wristwatch, it means a money loss in your business, depending on the circumstances. Buying a watch, peace and happiness. If they want to steal your watch and they can't, you'll face the problem; you'll have losses in business, but you'll recover. If a watch is gifted to a girl, it's a possible proposal for marriage. LN*51238, (1)

- Clock: If you buy it, good news in business. If it stops, you'll be out of the way of illness. LN*33632, (8)

Water: Drinking water out of a glass is good because it represents the purity if the water. If you can see through the glass and the water is clear, it represents prosperity. It can also be seen as a coming matrimony for someone who is in love or has a lover. Drinking dirty water means sickness. If the dreamer is sick, it's a worsening of their illness. LN*51259, (4)

- Drinking ice cold water represents success and triumph over any person or subject. Hot water is a bit negative. It may indicate you have problems with your enemies.

- Water: If you feel they are throwing water on your head or you yourself have poured water on your head, your head is related to your unconscious with which we think and do. It means fortune and financial improvement.

- Throwing water in the pool is also good luck. If the water is dirty, it means problems. Clear water means life is presenting you with great opportunities.

Waves: if they are normal as you always see them at sea it's a fortunate dream. If they are too strong and tall with a tendency to destroy, they're conflicts, if you are at sea in a boat. If the waves are huge and they destroy a town, this means big financial problems. LN*51451, (7)

Website: Seeing or checking a website, a desire to communicate with friends or loved ones. LN*5521925, (11)

Wedding: If you are single, this is positive in every way. If you are married, this means the contrary, family conflicts. If it is another person getting married, this is family happiness and benefits. LN*5544957, (12)

Wells: Fear of falling in life. If it's a man, his wife may be causing him some problems, rifts at home. The well is an empty space. Every empty space reflects problems and conflicts. If you fall in and you're unharmed, you'll come out okay from your problems. If you never reach the bottom, it's hard for you to realize who's causing you problems. LN*55331, (8)

White: Color of pureness, happiness in the family, and purification. It's good luck to dream about any object that is white, as well as animals, garments, and items. Success in all your projects, aspire for more. Good relationships with everyone. LN*58925, (2)

Whiskey: Possible illness, certain difficulties. Don't lend money; it'll be difficult to pay off things for some time. Offering whiskey to the person you love, you'll become thin. LN*5891257, (1)

Wings: Success if you decide to fly. Try it, you are ready. LN*59571, (9)

Wind: Better times, good news. Walking against the wind when it's strong and reaching your destination, success over your adversaries. LN*5954, (5)

Wise: Dreaming about a person you know is wise represents your need to not only learn and receive information but also advice. You may be going through a tough situation, and you'll have to make wise decisions. Look for people who know about the topic so you can make an informed decision. LN*5915, (2)

Wolf: If they attack you, great problems regarding your intrigues. If you kill one, you will beat your rival. If it protects you, loyal friends when you least expect them. LN*5636, (2)

Wound: It's not always bad unless you have internal bleeding and the blood stains your clothing. If it doesn't hurt, everything is under control. If you have a wound on your chest or heart, you are falling in love. If you have a wound on your nose, be very careful. You are losing your sense of smell; you are not seeing the source of the problem. LN*56354, (5)

Wound up: Internal fight. Speak with your internal you and agree to unwind yourself. LN*5635437, (6)

Worm: A caterpillar becoming a butterfly, success. Worm on the ground or in fruits, this is the negative part of us all. We have to change our negative way of seeing things. LN*5694, (6)

Worker/Blue collar worker: If it's in construction, growth of a project. In agriculture, residual income. Firing, contradictions. LN*569259, (9)

Wool: Protection from you towards someone else or the protection someone gives to you. Depends if you wrap yourself in wool or if you wrap someone else. Working with wool, gains. If you are gifted wool, you will be supported by good friends in your projects. LN*5663, (11)

Wrinkles: Don't pay too much attention if you are young and see yourself with wrinkles. If you are older, your older years worry you more than you think, not only physically but with other things that come with age. LN*59952351, (12)

Writing: Start of many things, change of lifestyle. (See autograph) Shows abilities not yet discovered. Talent of a poet. LN*5992957, (1)

Letter X

Letter X: As a symbol or letter, it represents that we are crossed, whether it points to events, circumstances or the people in your life. There are still thing to resolve. LN*(6)

XBOX: Related to manipulation on your part or you feel manipulated. LN*6266, (2)

Xfinity: Amplitude and at the same time rebuke, depending on if you have few or a lot of channels in your dream. LN*6695927, (8)

Letter Y

Yacht: The same as the boat. If the sea is not choppy, your ambitions will be achieved. If the sea is choppy, disappointment in love. LN*71382, (3)

Yellow: The color yellow represents mental qualities and power, the color of the sun (gold). If it is dark yellow, low passions. Light yellow, material stability. LN*753365, (2)

Youth: If you see yourself younger or older than your age, you are strong and wish to keep learning. You will start new projects that will require more time from you. LN*76328, (8)

Yoga: If you see yourself doing yoga easily, tranquility, stability, respect, and control. If you are not able to do the exercises because you're not flexible, you're being inflexible in life and fear is opening up new horizons. LN*7671, (21)

Letter Z

Zebra: Good and bad. You're going through moments in your life in which you don't know the right decision to make, especially if it's related to choosing a partner. LN*85291, (7)

Zoo: Good luck if you're visiting one. Seeing the animals outside of a zoo isn't good. LN*866, (2)

Zumba: Dream related to social activity. You wish to relate more and be more noticed. LN*83421, (9)

The Author
Ivania Alvarado

Ivania Alvarado

I was born in Mangua, Nicaragua. The eldest of three siblings, I believe in the five universal positions: one is God, the second is myself, the third my family, fourth my career, and fifth my positive pleasures.

I migrated to the United States when I was 20 years old. I put all my focus in my studies, graduating with several degrees: Real Estate, mortgage loans, real estate broker, Insurance agent, hypnosis, and other studies of less importance. I have a batchelor's degree in Supervision and Management-Accounting Concentration.

When I turned 24, I went into business ventures, opening my first corporation in the United States, managing a school for real estate, an insurance agency, and a securities firm that helped me create the *Real Estate Manual.* This book was the fundamental base for training seminars in this profession.

I have vast experience in education, promoting people, recruiting, training, advising, and educating sellers. The real estate company of five associates, under my direction, grew to one hundred and twenty associates, and graduated more than a thousand students at the South Florida School of Real Estate.

In the year 2000, I started creating for various patents and three inventions, two for design and one for utility. In 2001, I rebooted my literary qualities, writing a "Your Dreams and You" section for diverse magazines, taking me to the writing of my second book, *Your Dreams and You.*

In 2004, I was musically inspired to create a CD of lyrical music, composed with much care and dedication. In 2016, I began my career as a singer-songwriter with the album "Your Dreams and You" now for sale on Amazon and iTunes. I'm in the process of offering a new editorial and musical piece. I also created radio and television programs on the theme of the interpretation of dreams.

I find giving to religious institutions that help the homeless, Mother Teresa of Calcutta, the elderly, the hill, addicts and children with special conditions my most spiritually fulfilling contribution.

Visit my website for more information at: IvaniaAlvarado.com or sfsre.net.

Dreams diary and its use

I would like this diary to be useful so you can learn and practice for yourself the interpretation of your dreams.

Each day you write, record your own interpretations and create a positive habit.

If for any reason you don't remember your dream, start by writing how you feel when you wake up. That is the first step to remember. When you do this exercise over time, you'll develop a useful and healthy habit.

Remember there are many reasons why keeping a diary of your dreams is important:

- You can have a millionaire idea.
- You'll have a better connection with yourself.
- You'll know yourself better.
- Your conscience and subconscious will be aligned more easily when they confront each other.
- You'll be able to heal past wounds.
- You can decipher messages.
- Your dreams always work in your favor; make them work for you.
- It improves your memory.
- It's fun.
- It'll be something to share with your friends and family.
- For some it works like therapy.
- It can be a warning about adversity.
- It improves your creativity.
- You can evaluate your feelings.

- It's an exercise for your mind.
- And much more...

Secrets for your dreams diary to be successful.

Title your dream. Try to make it easy to identify, and describe in few words what you've dreamed. For example: "Dream was about yellow shoes."

Record the exact date and hour of the dream.

Write how you feel when you wake up.

Include pictures or drawings if you have them. For example, if you dreamed of a deceased family member, it's great if you can include a picture of that person.

Describe your feelings and sensations and ambience during the dream. Use very descriptive words, including details. Did it rain? Was it cold? Was it a sunny day?

Does the dream refer to past situations or the future?

Try to remember any dialogue or if you heard or think you heard voices with messages that communicated something special.

Describe the people in the dream. Were they family members, friends, or strangers?

Learn to control your mind. Before you go to sleep, perform small rituals that allow you to achieve a deep sleep that is healing and enjoyable.

Place the book, a notebook, and a pencil close to your bed or armchair, and promise yourself you'll write daily for at least seven days.

Remember, when you interpret your dreams using the tools I've given you, you can make your dreams come true!

Your Dreams and You

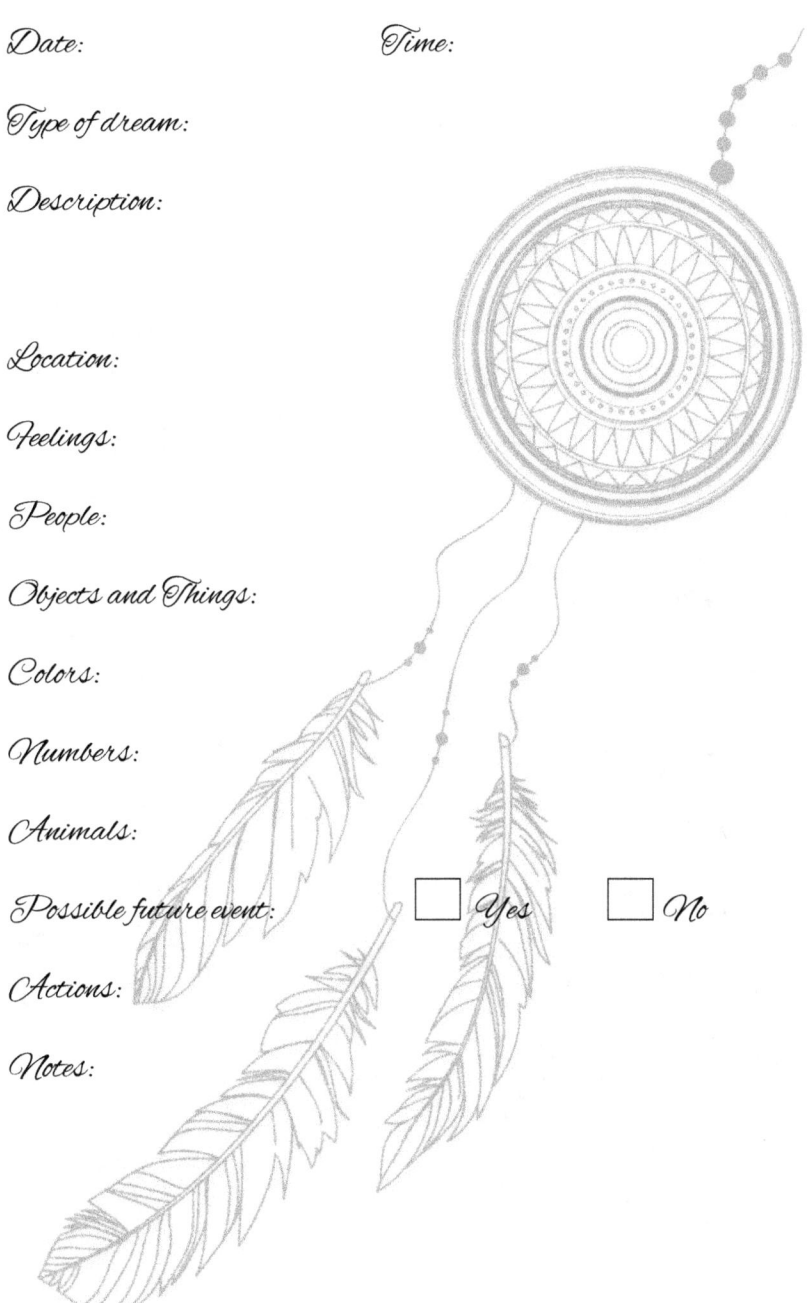

Date: Time:

Type of dream:

Description:

Location:

Feelings:

People:

Objects and Things:

Colors:

Numbers:

Animals:

Possible future event: ☐ Yes   ☐ No

Actions:

Notes:

Your Dreams and You

Date: Time:

Type of dream:

Description:

Location:

Feelings:

People:

Objects and Things:

Colors:

Numbers:

Animals:

Possible future event: ☐ Yes   ☐ No

Actions:

Notes:

Your Dreams and You

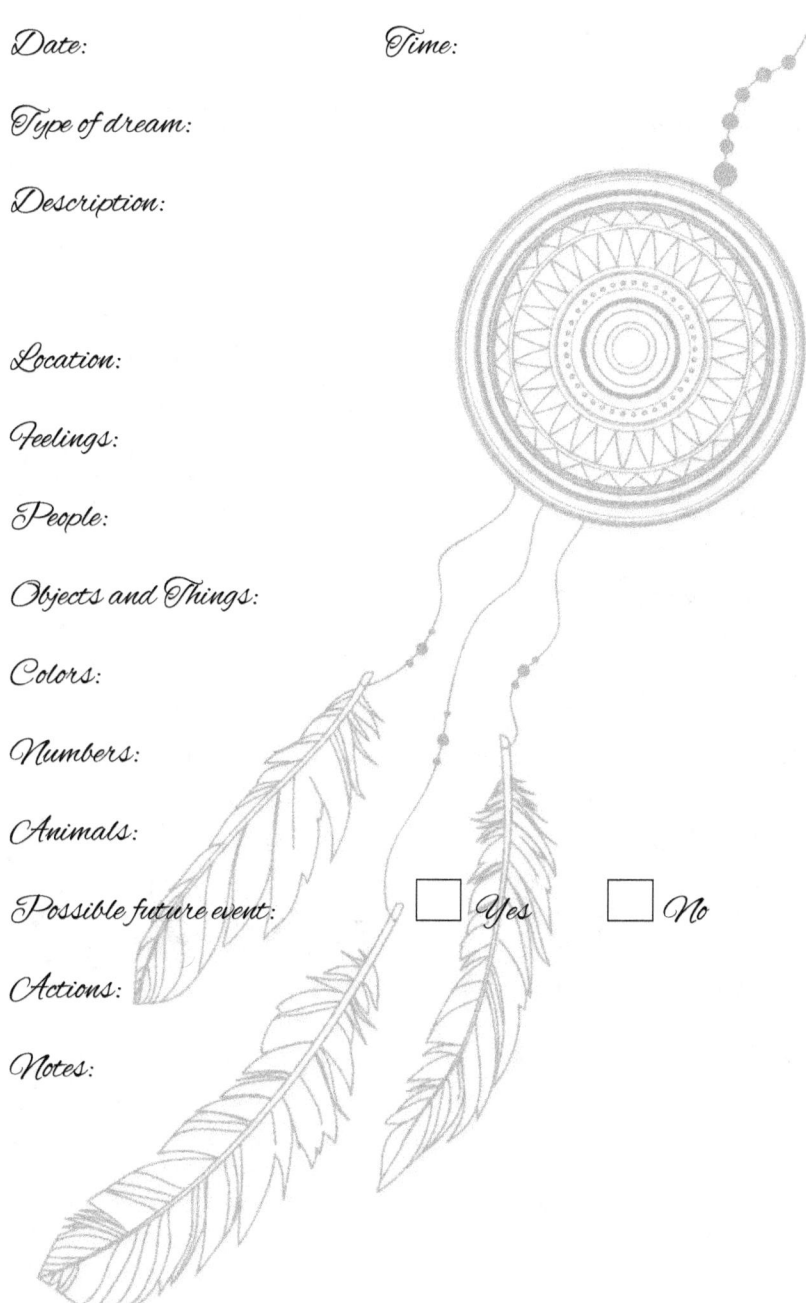

Date: Time:

Type of dream:

Description:

Location:

Feelings:

People:

Objects and Things:

Colors:

Numbers:

Animals:

Possible future event: ☐ Yes   ☐ No

Actions:

Notes:

Your Dreams and You

Date:

Time:

Type of dream:

Description:

Location:

Feelings:

People:

Objects and Things:

Colors:

Numbers:

Animals:

Possible future event: ☐ Yes ☐ No

Actions:

Notes:

Your Dreams and You

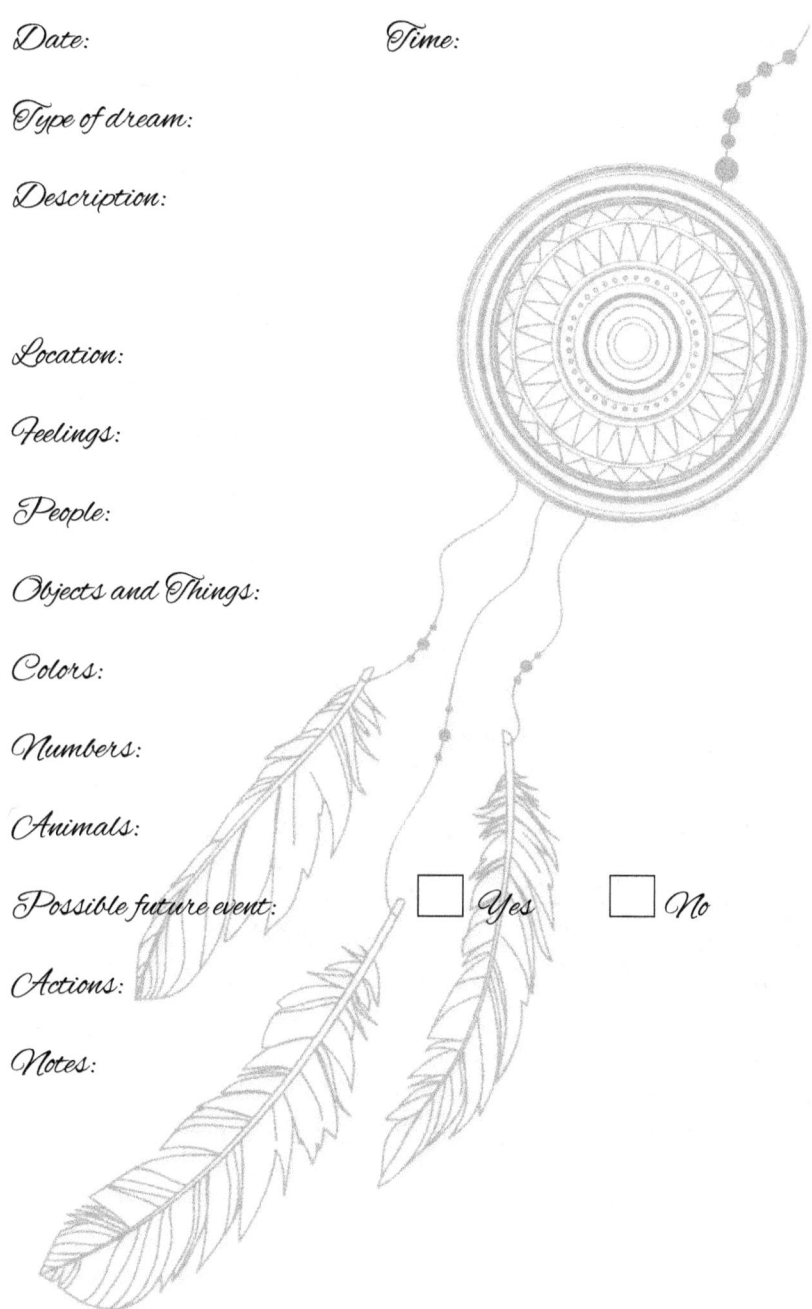

Date: Time:

Type of dream:

Description:

Location:

Feelings:

People:

Objects and Things:

Colors:

Numbers:

Animals:

Possible future event: ☐ Yes   ☐ No

Actions:

Notes:

Your Dreams and You

Date: Time:

Type of dream:

Description:

Location:

Feelings:

People:

Objects and Things:

Colors:

Numbers:

Animals:

Possible future event: ☐ Yes   ☐ No

Actions:

Notes:

Your Dreams and You

Date: Time:

Type of dream:

Description:

Location:

Feelings:

People:

Objects and Things:

Colors:

Numbers:

Animals:

Possible future event: ☐ Yes   ☐ No

Actions:

Notes:

Your Dreams and You

Date: Time:

Type of dream:

Description:

Location:

Feelings:

People:

Objects and Things:

Colors:

Numbers:

Animals:

Possible future event: ☐ Yes   ☐ No

Actions:

Notes:

Your Dreams and You

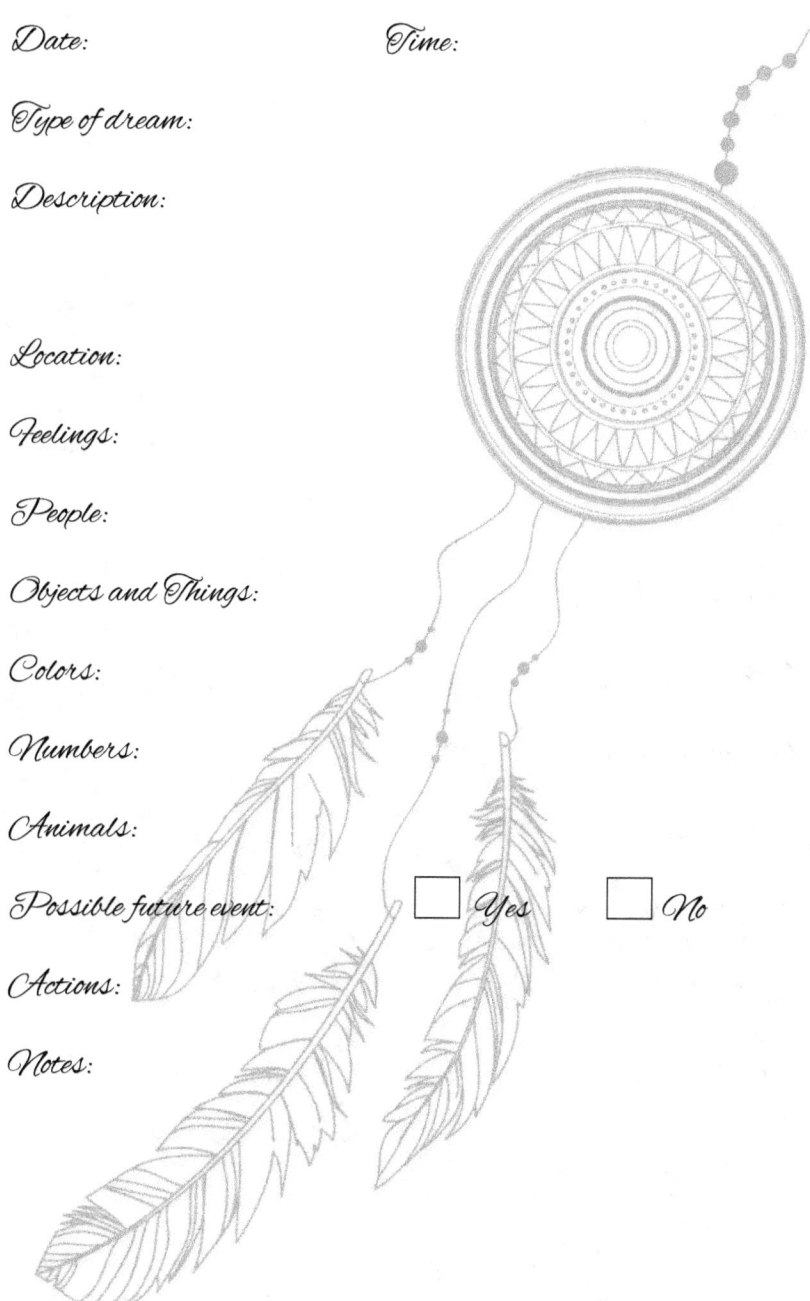

Date: Time:

Type of dream:

Description:

Location:

Feelings:

People:

Objects and Things:

Colors:

Numbers:

Animals:

Possible future event: ☐ Yes   ☐ No

Actions:

Notes:

Your Dreams and You

Date: Time:

Type of dream:

Description:

Location:

Feelings:

People:

Objects and Things:

Colors:

Numbers:

Animals:

Possible future event: ☐ Yes   ☐ No

Actions:

Notes:

Your Dreams and You

Date: Time:

Type of dream:

Description:

Location:

Feelings:

People:

Objects and Things:

Colors:

Numbers:

Animals:

Possible future event: ☐ Yes   ☐ No

Actions:

Notes:

Your Dreams and You

Date: Time:

Type of dream:

Description:

Location:

Feelings:

People:

Objects and Things:

Colors:

Numbers:

Animals:

Possible future event: ☐ Yes ☐ No

Actions:

Notes:

Your Dreams and You

Date: Time:

Type of dream:

Description:

Location:

Feelings:

People:

Objects and Things:

Colors:

Numbers:

Animals:

Possible future event: ☐ Yes   ☐ No

Actions:

Notes:

www.ingramcontent.com/pod-product-compliance
Lightning Source LLC
Chambersburg PA
CBHW071826080526
44589CB00012B/929